Brits on Route 66:

A Very British Guide to the World's Greatest Road Trip

Vicki Graves

First published in the United Kingdom in 2018 by Stage 25 Publishing

Contact and purchase information can be found at www.britsonroute66.co.uk

Inscription from the Survivor Tree reproduced with the permission of the Oklahoma City National Memorial and Museum.

Lillian Redman's benediction and quotes from www.blueswallowmotel.com reproduced with the permission of the Blue Swallow Motel.

Quotations from the Kevin the Tee Pee Curios Pooch Facebook page were reproduced with permission from the page.

Mentions of the *EZ66 Guide for Travelers* included with the permission of the author, Jerry McClanahan.

Cover image: Patsetubal/Shutterstock.com

This book is a travelogue. The author has tried to recreate events and conversations from their memories of them. Some details have been compressed, and some dialogue has been recreated. In some instances, details have been omitted to ensure privacy. The personal opinions contained within are not intended to hurt anyone, simply encourage more people to travel Route 66.

ISBN: 978 -1-9164334-0-3

For Grandad Colin – forever with me on life's adventures.

CONTENTS

1
ARE YOU UP FOR AN AMERICAN ADVENTURE?

We were star-struck. Standing on the sidewalk on a sunny September morning, with the warm Arizona tarmac beside us and an old barbershop in front, we couldn't believe our luck. Or barely open our mouths.

We'd arrived at Seligman early. We'd left the diners and neon signs of Williams – the last Route 66 town to be bypassed by the interstate – before 8 a.m., in the hope of beating the hordes of tourists to get a glimpse of Main Street undisturbed. We'd passed the famous Burma-Shave signs and laughed at the retro advertisements disguised as safety messages, painted onto red wooden boards along the roadside. We'd stopped to take a photo of the legendary 'Historic 66' shield, stencilled onto the tyre-stained concrete. Just us and our Dodge Challenger; we hadn't seen another vehicle for miles.

We'd parked our all-American muscle car (a little dusty from the desert sand) and walked over to the barbers, now a gift shop selling Route 66 merchandise. We'd paused to take photos of the Texaco sign and the retro pick-up that we'd seen countless times in books and artwork. And then he just walked out.

To anyone else, to those unfamiliar with the highway's history, he may have been just an ordinary pensioner. An old man wearing a hearing aid, straightening one of the flags hanging from his shop that had become tangled in the wind. But to us, he was a real-life superhero. Living history. Angel Delgadillo, the man who saved this legendary road and made our entire trip possible. A man who so few roadies are lucky enough to meet, was standing right in front of us, on his way home before the throngs of tour buses and bikers arrived. Dave, my now husband, was brave enough to shake his hand. I just gawped in awe.

Because that's what Route 66 does to you. It has you gobsmacked at meeting a shopkeeper in his nineties before you've even had your breakfast. It has you drive for hours across beaten-up road surfaces to look at a statue of a kid who ran more than 3,000 miles from Los Angeles (LA) to New York. It has you giddy at the thought of the world's second largest rocking chair (that doesn't actually rock) or the sight of a giant blue whale that some guy built as an anniversary present for his wife. It makes you feel part of a very special community, a wondrous piece of Americana that straddles past and present. It combines adventure with absurdity, nostalgia with self-discovery. If you let it, it can change your life.

Route 66, 2,448 miles of retro motels, souvenir shops, roadside giants and even a president's house, is so much more than the world's most famous road trip. Stretching between Chicago and Santa Monica, the bucket-list favourite passes through eight states and three time zones. Dubbed the 'Will Rogers Highway', on account of the beloved actor who helped to promote it, the road has captured the hearts of countless filmmakers, novelists, songwriters and tourists. Each person who journeys its length develops a unique and personal relationship with the highway, interpreting its symbolism around their own ideals.

To Dave and me, Route 66 was to be our ultimate adventure. A chance to feel truly free, exploring a different town almost every day. A journey of a lifetime that would take us through the heart of the USA on the open road. A trip for us to indulge in our love of art deco architecture and 1950s retro, to eat delicious calorific food, take detours to marvel at the Grand Canyon and experience the bright lights of Las Vegas. A perfect way to marry Dave's passion for driving with my longing to travel and explore such a complex and expansive country.

But we didn't expect to become completely absorbed by the road, fascinated by its culture and people. We loved staying up until the early hours planning our trip, consumed in guidebooks and internet forums and watching every documentary we could find. There were telephone chats with motel owners across the pond, who couldn't wait for us to visit, and social media conversations with people (and sometimes even their pets) we'd never met, but whose stories captivated us.

Because it's difficult not to become just a little bit obsessed with Route 66. In travelling it, you become somehow intertwined with the road (although not literally, I hope…). You become connected to its culture and part of its ever-evolving, and very much living, history.

It's a legacy that started way back in the 1920s. With motor cars becoming increasingly popular, there became a desperate need to improve the road network, which was currently little more than a collection of dirt tracks. States across the US began creating a series of interstate highways, connecting towns and cities throughout the country. Route 66 sprang from this movement, linking together a number of existing paths, only 800 miles of which were paved. Work began on the rest in 1926 and it took until 1937 to complete.

The road was planned and championed by Oklahoma resident Cyrus Avery, President of the Associated Highways Associations of America. Avery gave the road its name, promotional slogan – 'The Main Street of America' – and sought to promote it through an onslaught of advertising campaigns, including everything from a logo to PR stunts. Perhaps the most famous of these was the 1928 International Trans-Continental Foot Race – touted by tabloids as the Bunion Derby – a 3,423.5-mile ultra-marathon from LA to New York (I'll save more on that fascinating story until later).

By the 1930s, Route 66 came to signify something all the more terrifying – the Dust Bowl. Beginning in 1934, severe droughts met with strong winds and whipped up clouds of dust that cloaked the sky for almost a decade. In towns across Oklahoma and Texas, as well as those in the adjoining sections of Kansas, Colorado and New Mexico, houses were buried in mountains of dust – some up to their roofs – torn up from the barren landscape and failed agricultural fields. Families lived under blackened skies, with visibility sometimes reduced to just one metre.

The harsh conditions, coupled with the economic gloom of the Great Depression, forced thousands of farming families to flee their homes, abandoning their land to travel west in the hope of a better future. For many it was 'California or bust'. It's the story depicted in John Steinbeck's *The Grapes of Wrath*, where broken 'Okies' took to the 'Mother Road' to find work in the fruit farms of the Golden State, only to be met with further hardship. In the following years, the Second World War saw the route lined with military vehicles, carrying soldiers and supplies across the USA.

But it's the decade that came after the war that produced perhaps the most famous image of Route 66 in modern consciousness. The years evoked whenever someone hears Bobby Troup's iconic anthem, composed in 1946. The same year that Jack Rittenhouse published *A Guide Book to Highway 66*, signalling the start of the great American road trip down Main Street USA. The 1940s and 1950s were the times of diners, neon signs, family vacations, drive-in movies and roadside attractions.

This was the Route 66 heyday, but sadly also the start of its demise. Influenced by the German autobahn, President Eisenhower passed the Federal Aid Highway Act in 1956, kick-starting the national interstate system which would eventually see the entire length of the road bypassed. US 66 had become so popular it was struggling to cope with the large amounts of traffic it attracted and, in 1985, the highway was formally decommissioned. Signs were taken down and businesses on the route began to collapse, some within a day.

But like all good stories, there was a guardian angel. Two years after Route 66 was finally sent to the highway graveyard, one man fought to bring it back from the dead – Angel Delgadillo, the man Dave and I were so excited to meet. Born and raised in Seligman and owner of the town's barbershop, Angel got mad when he found out that authorities had removed signage pointing to his town after the decommissioning of the road. In 1987, nine years after the interstate bypassed Seligman, Angel and his pals formed the Historic Route 66 Association of Arizona and lobbied the state to replace the signs and recognise the stretch of 66 running through his state as a historic highway. His success saw others along the route form their own associations, leading to the rebirth of the road and its renewed appeal across the world to people like Dave and me.

That's why we were elated to shake Angel's hand on that Seligman morning, to see his kind eyes light up as he welcomed us – two complete strangers – into the shop he'd worked so hard to maintain. To meet someone who, in changing his own small corner of the world, had literally paved the way for so many others to create their own adventures, was amazing. To look at the warmth on his face was to imagine countless memories of a life lived on a road that brought so much joy to so many people, each flashing past in an instant, like a Polaroid slideshow. The feeling was magical.

But, of course, it's not just the efforts of Angel and his colleagues that are responsible for the 66 we know today. In 2006, Pixar's animated masterpiece, *Cars*, brought the tale of the road's rise and fall (and rise once again) to millions of children and their parents; many of the characters, and even the scenery, are heavily based on real people, buildings and attractions. Once you've travelled the highway, you won't be able to watch the film without spotting yet another one of its influences – the movie is nothing short of genius in my opinion. I'm not so keen on the sequels.

And then there's the internet. Websites, forums and, perhaps most importantly, social media, connect Route 66ers across the globe. They all help restaurateurs and motel owners to promote their businesses cheaply and easily in a way that just wasn't possible pre-1991.

It's this continual reinvention, this refusal to let something valued fade away, that represents what Route 66 signifies for me. Survival. The road is endurance. Its people are fighters who won't give up on their quest to get more from life – the American Dream. It's a spirit that struck me the moment I started reading about the road. One present ever since Avery fought for its creation to improve the road network and the prospects of his home state (Oklahoma), right through to Angel's revival campaign and beyond. It's one of the reasons I think about the road, and our adventure on it, almost every day.

The lesson is one I think many people can learn from. Just because somebody may write you off, or consign you to the past, doesn't mean you have to take it lying down. When the authorities removed the 66 shields and erased the highway from their maps, the people of the Mother Road stood up and fought for what was theirs. They rallied together and changed history, not to lament the past but to protect their futures. And just like those shopkeepers and moteliers, if you want something, you too can fight for it. If you try hard enough, you can succeed. It just takes hard work and a little help from your friends.

And you'll find plenty of pals along Route 66. The highway is a family of travellers and business owners looking to share their stories, always there to support one another. A cafe cook in Kansas might be best friends with a garage proprietor in Missouri, connected via the telephone and the World Wide Web. These people are what make travelling the road such a joy and an individual experience. You can make friendships that last a lifetime. So be prepared to welcome these strangers, sit a while and listen to their tales and share a few of your own. This is the only way to truly experience the highway's magic.

But don't expect glamour, glitz or luxury. The neon lights that once shone brightly are gone from many motels. Their windows are boarded up, their buildings left to rot and their gas (the US word for petrol) pumps covered with rust. As fast as some communities can restore their Main Streets, many have become little more than ghost towns. Attractions open, close and change owners regularly (so check before you travel). The romantic image of 66 as a beacon of fifties Americana is often just an imaginary ideal. It's true today in some places, but certainly not in others.

The route has a dark side too. Guidebooks delineate some areas as not safe for tourists. On one night we spent in Chicago, a police officer was shot dead. In another town, we overheard racist conversations, in broad daylight, whilst eating our lunch. And the subtle sexism I experienced in an Illinois bar didn't go unnoticed by Dave or me. In one motel, the lady behind the counter asked if we were on our honeymoon. When I send 'no', she looked at my ringless finger (at the time) and simply replied 'oh' before checking us into our double room. The Bible Belt is an interesting stretch – and don't forget that 66 drives straight through the heart of Tornado Alley.

This darker undercurrent has existed from the road's inception, and arguably even before. After all, Springfield, Illinois is still home to Abraham Lincoln's house, the US president who campaigned against slavery in the Civil War. In St Louis, Missouri, the Gateway Arch marks the beginning of the expansion into the Wild West, where advancing cowboys battled with Native American Indians. From the 1930s to the 1960s, Victor H. Green published *The Negro Motorist Green Book* because travelling on roads like 66 was often fraught with prejudice and double standards, making journeying them less than pleasant for many black families. And there's the road's nickname of 'Bloody 66', earned because of its dangerous road surfaces in places during bad weather, traffic volumes and more difficult stretches, like the Oatman Highway, back in the road's heyday.

I mention these more negative elements because they are important, but also for balance. You must examine both the good and the bad in order to truly understand Route 66's place in American history. But in truth, any negative instances were few and far between for us, and our decision to journey its length was one of the best we've ever made. The people of the road are some of the friendliest and most hospitable we've ever met, and their compassion is genuine not just for the sale.

Travelling Route 66 is an unforgettable experience and one I believe more of us should indulge in. The road is the best way to see America's landscape change as you drive across it. In speaking to its people and visiting its museums, there are important lessons in culture, politics and, above all, understanding and tolerance.

You'll see amazing buildings, modern historical relics, wonders of nature, deserted towns and odd, but fantastic, roadside attractions. You'll experience art, music and literature and meet people that make you feel right at home, though you're thousands of miles away. You'll have conversations that you'll remember forever, some that may even change your point of view.

This book tells my story of driving the Mother Road as a Brit with my partner (now husband) and will hopefully inspire you to embark on a trip of your own. You won't find step-by-step directions (you need the *EZ Guide* for that), but you will find my thoughts on the places we visited and stayed during our vacation, along with handy advice for those travelling from outside the USA (particularly the UK) which I found was lacking when we were planning our journey.

So read my ramblings, book your flights and become part of Route 66's vibrant history. You won't regret it.

2
THE WORLD'S GREATEST ROAD TRIP? NOW THAT'S A PLAN!

I'm a planner. I like lists, charts and generally being organised. Just call me Monica Bing. A few months before we flew to Chicago, one of my colleagues commented that Dave and I had put so much time and effort into planning our trip that he wondered if we'd enjoy the holiday to its full potential. To him, road trips are about being spontaneous. What would we do if things didn't go to plan?

I have to admit I was worried. We'd spent two years researching Route 66 and knew exactly what we wanted to see and when we wanted to see it. Would our months spent reading and searching the internet make things less exciting when we finally got to America? Had we spoilt the trip for ourselves by being too prepared?

Fast-forward to a September's evening in Holbrook, Arizona. Dave and I had just finished two big plates of New Mexican food at the famous Joe and Aggie's Cafe when one of the employees (who turned out to be the grandson of the original owners) began telling another couple about the restaurant's history. Dave and I joined them and, more than an hour later, the other couple having long since left, we were still standing at the cash register talking about Route 66, the places we'd been to and the towns we were yet to see. We were given presents – branded casino chips reserved only for Joe and Aggie's 'special friends' – recommended attractions to visit and told personal stories about the Mother Road from people that live on it day in and day out.

The treatment and hospitality we experienced at Joe and Aggie's was the rule rather than the exception. In every town we visited, the more we showed our passion for 66, the more its community wanted to share their stories with us.

So rather than draining the spontaneity from our trip, our prior research made our travels even more enjoyable. It gave us the knowledge, and the confidence, to engage in more meaningful conversations with the people that dedicate their lives to the road every day. It's these experiences that make driving Route 66 such a personal experience, with the people that you meet and the interactions you have with them defining your trip.

And let's not forget, travelling almost 2,500 miles, across multiple states and time zones, is one epic journey – one that really should take some prior thought. You'll encounter desert landscape, rough road surfaces and, potentially, life-threatening wildlife. A little preparation goes a long way.

When to go?

Avoid winter (January to March), July and August. In the height of the American summer, temperatures in the desert region can be stifling. July and August also mark peak season, so expect long queues, higher ticket prices and lots of tourists and their children enjoying their summer breaks.

From November into winter, temperatures drop, and it even snows in some states. Areas of the road become dangerous and off-limits, especially Arizona's Oatman Highway and the mountain routes in New Mexico and California. These stretches have some of the best views on Route 66, so it really would be a shame to miss them. Similarly, many attractions shut between October and April or reduce their opening hours.

Tornado season runs from March to June too. With America's Main Street cruising straight through Tornado Alley, you might want to think carefully about travelling during these months.

We drove Route 66 in September. Our flights were cheaper because the UK school holidays were over, and the weather was more comfortable than tackling the desert in the summer. We encountered rain, and a little hail, but when driving cross-country through changing landscape, some precipitation is to be expected. We had sunny days too, and the heat in LA and Las Vegas was warming (around 20°C) without being overbearing.

There's no perfect time to drive Route 66, but book your travel between May and late September and you should enjoy the best of the sunshine and avoid the worst of the extreme weather.

Drive west, or east?

It's not just the Dust Bowl that made westward travel on 66 famous. In the 1950s and 1960s, the height of the American road-trip era saw an abundance of families journeying west along the highway, seeking the bright lights and fireworks of Disneyland, sampling countless roadside attractions on the way. As such, east to west signals the 'traditional' Route 66 adventure, starting in Chicago and ending in Santa Monica, LA. It was our chosen direction of travel and is the default of many guidebooks (including this one), coach trips and package deals.

Heading east has its advantages too, and many travellers even prefer it. This is a one-way trip for most adventurers, especially us foreigners, so you may find a greater choice of cars in LA. If you're thinking of combining your road trip with a journey down America's coastal Highway One (lucky you!), San Francisco would make a fantastic starting point.

Route 66 is an unforgettable, individual experience, regardless of which way you travel it. So choose your own direction.

Self-guided or organised trip?

The decision whether to book a guided tour, package deal or research and plan the trip yourself depends on many factors – budget, how much freedom you desire and not least your confidence in driving.

Coach trips and guided tours can be great ways to see the road and its attractions if you want the security of travelling in a group or don't want the work of researching what to see and when. Often contrary to public perception, modern-day Route 66 is not one long, continuous road. Over its 59-year history, before it was finally decommissioned in 1985, the road was continually re-routed, rebuilt and re-organised to make way for increased traffic volumes, create shortcuts and, often, because its concrete had simply fallen into disrepair.

This means that drivers of today's Route 66 will have to make decisions over which alignments to follow, for example whether to take the longer pre-1937 route through the Santa Fe hills or follow the more modern trail straight to Albuquerque, not to mention the many off-shoots of original dirt road. Add the fact that many sections of the road have been replaced by interstate, have deteriorated so much that they are impassable, or have simply been renamed and you'll understand why many people say that following the Mother Road can be difficult at times. Some states have tried to make the journey easier by marking the route with signs and arrows, but unfortunately these are often the victims of theft. If this sounds like a lot of hassle to you, a supervised trip with an organised guide is probably the way to go.

If you don't want to travel as part of a group, but don't fancy the planning involved in a self-guided trip, a self-drive package holiday provides a handy compromise. Since the release of *Cars* and the airing of documentaries like Billy Connolly's *Route 66*, self-drive tours down America's Main Street are becoming frequent additions to the brochures of mainstream travel operators. Virgin Holidays, First Class Holidays and Thomas Cook are just three of the many companies that offer off-the-shelf packages, organising your car, hotels and itinerary. These can often be cheaper than planning and booking your trip yourself and get around some of the restrictions of travelling by coach (or RV). For example, some segments of Route 66, such as the fantastic, but very windy and narrow, Oatman Highway, are not advisable to travel in long vehicles. However, package trips are often limited to 14 or 16 days and, although they provide the freedom of putting the pedal to the metal yourself, you will still largely be limited to a pre-defined itinerary.

A self-guided tour will provide the greatest degree of freedom, and this is the option Dave and I chose. We didn't want to be restricted by having to get up at a particular time or eat at a particular restaurant. We wanted to choose the motels we slept in, determine how long we stayed at each attraction and eat at the times we wanted to, in the places we wanted to eat in. By planning the trip ourselves, we were able to add on detours to the Grand Canyon and Las Vegas and visit lesser known spots, such as the Oklahoma National Stockyards (I'm a tad obsessed by cows). We were also able to determine the length of our trip (23 days), and it gave us the freedom to add in extra stops along the way after hearing recommendations from the people we met en route. With a little preparation, we also managed to follow the route from start to finish (more or less), getting lost only once or twice.

However, I am glad we opted for the car instead of a motorbike. As well as restricting the amount of luggage you can carry, and therefore the amount of souvenirs you can collect along the way, we met lots of couples on Harleys who were having trouble navigating the road. Whilst I could check directions and, attempt to, read the map in transit from the comfort of the passenger's seat, our motorbike pals frequently had to pull over to determine their next move, and we often saw them making a wrong turn. The result was that they missed sections of Historic Route 66, opting instead for the ease of the interstate. Although I imagine cruising the road on two wheels would be exhilarating (especially the hilly sections in California), you need to be prepared for extra complications. A way around these navigational difficulties could be to opt for an organised bike tour. Of course you make a compromise in terms of freedom over your itinerary, but I'm sure that travelling as part of a gang of bikers would be an unforgettable experience.

Self-drive, but what to drive?

If you've decided to take the plunge and drive the trip yourself (good for you), you'll need to choose your mode of transport. Cars, RVs and motorbikes are all popular choices and each has its own pros and cons.

For a lot of people, the only way to ride the iconic American road trip is leather-clad and windswept on the saddle of a Harley-Davidson. For Dave and me, a motorbike was not a desirable option – we encountered flash flooding and storms on our journey across the US, so the warmth and dryness of our sports car was much appreciated.

However, I can see why a bike would be appealing. Riding that close to the asphalt through the curves and bumps of the road must be a lot of fun. There's also a real social element to being a biker on 66, especially if you are part of an organised tour, with those travelling the road in this way flocking towards each other in biker bars and motels in the evenings to discuss cylinders and horsepower over a few beers. It can be a great way to experience Route 66, provided you are prepared for some potential navigational issues.

Travelling by RV offers another completely different experience. We met a couple right at the start of our trip who had chosen a campervan for their steed and, looking at their holiday snaps on Facebook, their trip contrasted to ours in lots of ways. Whilst we ate in diners and slept in motels, they spent time in RV parks warming round campfires and chowing down on BBQ food. And that may be what you'll end up doing most nights if you opt for an RV – campsites are often outside of the main metropolis areas, so you'll need to drive to get to them, meaning alcohol is off-limits.

We opted for the traditional all-American muscle car, a bright red Dodge Challenger (which we hired from Alamo). The car of choice for many of our fellow travellers appeared to be the Mustang (I lost count of how many Brits we saw driving them). The famous Ford was also our preferred choice, but our hire company didn't havc any available when we went to upgrade and, ultimately, we were glad to be a little different; the Dodge Challenger isn't as common as a form of tourist transport (the only others we saw were driven by American residents, although we did chat to a French-Canadian couple who had crossed the border in theirs, but it was the one they owned and drove at home). Also, the Dodge had a lot more boot space than the

Mustang, so we didn't need to travel with luggage on the back seats.

For the most part, you'll be at the liberty of whichever hire company you choose as your car will depend on their fleet. We found that you couldn't book a 'muscle car' in advance – some companies can be reluctant to have their best vehicles travel to the other side of the country because they are unlikely to get another person to drive them back. So plan to upgrade when you arrive if you really want that special ride. Upgrade prices will vary, but, at the time of writing, I found that you could rent a Dodge Challenger for around $185 (approximately £131) a day from Alamo at LAX Airport, so this may be useful as an indicative cost. By comparison, non-sports car models ranged from around $35 to $106 (£25 to £75) a day from Chicago O'Hare. Rates are likely to fluctuate, so do you research.

If you're looking for a vintage muscle car, expect to pay a lot more. The Cadillacs and Mustangs of the 1950s and 1960s are beautiful, but rare, so their rates can be upwards of $400 (£284) a day (2018).

What to bring

What you decide to take with you is completely up to you, but here's a list of things that helped us out:

Essentials

- A credit card – a lot of the pay-at-pump gas stations, along with some motels, will only accept credit rather than debit cards. Do bear in mind though that not all UK credit cards are accepted in the USA, and limitless cards can be blocked at gas pumps, so do some research. This will also help ensure you get the best deal possible; some credit cards offer commission-free purchases or withdrawals in the USA, for example. Make sure you call your bank before you leave to tell them you will be abroad to avoid any unnecessary difficulties with your card being blocked.

- *The EZ66 Guide for Travelers* – Jerry McClanahan, the book's author, is a Route 66 legend. His book is generally regarded as the definitive step-by-step guide to following the road, and most would not attempt to travel it without it (I suggest you don't either). It includes turn-by-turn directions for travelling both east and westwards, along with handy maps and recommendations for attractions, lodging, restaurants and useful background information on a range of Route 66 must-sees.
- Sat nav – I must stress, you *should not* attempt to follow Route 66 by sat nav (unless you have installed all of the way points onto the device yourself). We met a couple doing the route who couldn't see what all the fuss was about. We soon found out they'd been following their sat nav and had spent the entire journey on the interstate. They'd missed a whole lot of Route 66 goodness as they hadn't been on the original road at all. Route 66 was decommissioned as a US highway, so most sat navs will not have the exact journey plotted and will simply divert you onto the major roads. That said, we found a sat nav invaluable as a sort-of digital map. We had it on at all times (apart from when it died upon entering Arizona, prompting slight panic), which helped us check we were still going the right way (Route 66 can be difficult to follow) and anticipate exactly where we needed to turn next. It was also useful in directing us to Las Vegas, a detour from Route 66.

- Sunglasses – the Arizona desert can be pretty reflective, so opt for polarised lenses.
- Printouts of your hotel reservations and tickets for any pre-booked attractions.
- An ESTA – anyone travelling to the USA from the UK (or any other country participating in the Visa Waiver Program (VWP)) is required to complete a visa waiver form (an ESTA) at least 72 hours before they fly. If you don't do this, you won't be allowed into the country (although an ESTA is no guarantee you will get through the border). These last for two years, so you will want to apply nearer to your departure date, but I suggest applying at least a month before in case there are any issues. ESTAs can be purchased online for around $14 (around £10 in 2018). You do not need to print it, but I always do. If you are travelling from a country outside the VWP, check USA immigration requirements.
- A mobile phone with data – no guidebook can be as current as internet news and forums. We found that some road names had changed since our copy of the *EZ Guide* was published, not to mention the fact that a 100-mile stretch of the road was shut when we were travelling, forcing us to take a detour. A quick check online and we discovered that the road had collapsed due to recent flash floods, and we were able to find another route. We purchased a pay-as-you-go SIM from Three, which enabled us to use our UK data package at no extra cost in the USA and was available at the time of writing.
- Clothes – pack for all weather, including rain. It can be cold in the desert at night, and if you

plan to hike in the Grand Canyon, you'll need walking boots.

Nice-to-haves

- *Rand McNally Road Atlas* – to be honest, we didn't really use this because the sat nav was helpful enough. However, if something goes wrong, you get lost or your sat nav dies like ours did, a map can be a lifesaver. It was a relatively inexpensive purchase from Amazon so I don't think you can be too prepared.
- *EZ Guide* maps – Jerry McClanahan also created a series of state maps to accompany his book, which can be purchased in addition online. We didn't really use them on our trip, but the maps really are works of art in their own right, complete with lots of charming illustrations, so we kept them as souvenirs.
- International Driving Permit (IDP) – this is not required by law in any of the Route 66 states, but we applied for one anyway to make things easier if we were pulled over for any reason. A lot of insurance companies will insist on seeing one if you have any issues, so it's worth paying the £5.50 for one from the Post Office (UK), or looking for one online if you live outside the UK.
- Not really something to pack, but a suggestion for how to pack. Consider taking a small hand-luggage sized suitcase with your overnight essentials. This way you can simply take this into your hotel each night, rather than lug your large suitcase up flights of stairs.

How much should I budget?

Just how much it will cost to travel Route 66 depends on many things, including the duration of your trip, the type of vehicle you choose, the type of accommodation you opt for and the activities you want to undertake whilst you're away.

However, I thought it would be helpful for you to know about two areas in particular:

- One-way car drop-off fee – like most Route 66 travellers, if you are returning your vehicle on the opposite side of the country from where you originally rented it, you will incur a drop-off fee of around £300 to £400 ($423 to $563) depending on supplier (2018), as well as any local taxes in the drop-off state. The only way to avoid this fee is to swap vehicles at every state border, but I would strongly advise against this. Much of 66 is rural landscapes and small towns, so expect to waste time with lengthy detours to the larger towns and cities every time you need to locate a car rental office. In my opinion, this time would be better spent exploring the true Route 66, and any monetary saving is likely to be counter-productive.
- Flights – if you're travelling from Britain, flying one-way to two different airports, for example flying into Chicago O'Hare and leaving from LAX, will be more expensive than return flights (this has something to do with UK aviation taxes apparently). You could consider booking an internal US flight back to your starting destination at the end of your trip and catching your return flight home from there, although this will require some extra planning. It is also worth checking out Norwegian Air as it offers

'budget' flights from Chicago O'Hare and LAX.

Should I book accommodation in advance?

Route 66 is undergoing a resurgence of interest, especially with those travelling from overseas, so if you plan to travel over the peak summer months, you would be wise to pre-book the majority of your accommodation before leaving home. Off-peak travel is a different story. We travelled in September, and although we had booked all of our rooms in advance, once we'd spent some time on the road, we quickly came to the conclusion that, for the most part, we needn't have bothered.

There is one very important exception here. If you plan to stay in some of the most iconic motels and hotels, you must book these in advance, no matter when you travel. Places like the Blue Swallow Motel in Tucumcari, the Wigwam Motel in Holbrook and the El Tovar in the Grand Canyon are extremely popular and get booked up quickly, so make sure you get a reservation as soon as you have booked your flights (airlines usually release these 11 months in advance).

We booked our accommodation and flights with a local travel agent – Fred Olsen Travel, who used First Class Holidays – and we found this significantly cheaper than booking everything separately ourselves. There were some hotels that they couldn't source for us, such as the Blue Swallow, because many of the most famous motels on the route prefer to deal with the travellers themselves rather than negotiate with agents. This wasn't a problem – Fred Olsen allowed us to make our own arrangement with these two or three motels, meaning we got to stay everywhere we wanted to.

What about gas?

As a general rule, view half a tank as empty and allow for the fact that the next gas station may be out of fuel. There are a few places on Route 66 where this is particularly important:

- There are only a couple of gas stations between Seligman and Kingman. Do not leave either town without a full tank.
- On the Kingman to Needles stretch, there is no gas station until Needles (70 miles).
- After Needles, the next gas station is 40 miles away in Fenner.
- After Fenner, the next gas station is also 40 miles away in Amboy.

Distances are westbound and approximate. We were also surprised to find that you pay for your fuel before filling up in the USA.

Storms, snakes and creepy crawlies

Route 66 weaves through Tornado Alley (you'll see plenty of tornado sirens along the roadside. Hopefully you won't hear any go off). Although you'd be sensible to time your trip to avoid tornado season, you'd do well to familiarise yourself with what to do if you were so unlucky that one did strike. There is lots of advice online, but important points to remember are not to drive in storm weather (even flash floods can sweep your car away in seconds) and 'tornado watch' means that conditions are favourable for a tornado, but one has not yet been spotted, whereas 'tornado warning' means severe weather is imminent. Listen to local radio stations if you are concerned, as this is where alerts are sounded.

Lightning storms are frequent in the Grand Canyon – we saw one from the comfort of the hotel's bar balcony, and it was spectacular. Awe-inspiring though they may be, they are dangerous if you are caught out hiking, or are even walking around the rim. People have been known to die as a result of strikes. Although I hope you will not have any issues, it is worth reading up on what to do in the event of a lightning storm. Great advice can be found on the Grand Canyon's website.

We were fortunate not to see any snakes during our journey (although we did spot tarantulas and a scorpion from the comfort of our car), but our friends travelling by RV did. Although the chances of running into a rattlesnake are pretty low if you stick to the towns, they do frequent the Arizona and California deserts and are known to sun themselves on the tarmac during summer evenings. If you do spot one, remain calm and walk carefully back away so as not to alarm it. There is plenty of advice online as to how to avoid and correctly treat snake bites, so I'd recommend a quick read, for peace of mind if nothing else.

US driving laws

A couple of quick pointers on US driving laws:

- You are required to come to a complete stop at every stop sign.
- At many traffic lights it is legal (and often required if you don't want horns beeping at you) to turn right on a red light. However, not all lights permit right turns on red, so look out for traffic signs.
- Not that you'll be speeding, but speeding fines are doubled in work zones (roadworks) in most states.
- There are also state-specific laws, so brush up on these before you leave.

You should also remember that Route 66 is a

decommissioned highway, so you can't rely on perfect road surfaces. In severe weather, some sections may even be impassable. So you need to drive carefully. The above advice was correct at the time of writing, but driving laws change. To be safe, check before you travel.

Time zones

Route 66 passes through three time zones, so you'll need to adjust your watch several times on your journey:

- Central Time Zone – Illinois, Missouri, Kansas, Oklahoma and Texas.
- Mountain Time Zone (one hour earlier) – New Mexico and Arizona.
- Pacific Time Zone (one hour earlier) – California (and Nevada).

NB: these are westward journey times.

Any other words of wisdom?

- Keep your mobile phone charged up and keep your car rental details in your vehicle in case of any issues.
- A tip of at least 15 per cent is usually expected in restaurants in the USA.
- Keep a crate of water and some snacks in your boot.

Other suggested reading

We found the following books invaluable for planning our trip:

- Jerry McClanahan – *EZ66 Guide for Travelers.*
- Tom Synder – *Route 66 Traveler's Guide and Roadside Companion.*

- Michael Wallis – *Route 66 The Mother Road* (this makes for a really beautiful coffee-table book too).
- Billy Connolly – *Billy Connolly's Route 66: The Big Yin on the Ultimate American Road Trip* (you should also watch the documentary series).

So now you're adequately prepared for the road ahead, let's go on a journey, state by state. In the following chapters you'll find my personal, tried and tested, recommendations of where to stay, what to see and who you should try to meet in each Route 66 destination, woven through the tale of mine and Dave's fantastic trip. I can't wait to share it with you.

3
GIANT BUILDINGS AND BIG HEARTS AT THE START OF THE ILLINOIS OPEN ROAD

Chicago in September is a place of opposites. When we drove into its Magnificent Mile district early Saturday evening, the city was bustling. I was struck by how noisy everything was. Amongst the giant towers, upmarket restaurants and trendy bars on this 13-block stretch of North Michigan Avenue, ambulances screeched and trains clattered on elevated tracks above the road. Even the music coming from our hotel lobby was loud.

But by Sunday morning, Chicago was deadly quiet. The city was almost deserted as we walked to Do-Rite Donuts & Coffee (50 W Randolph St) to satisfy both my sweet tooth and wheat intolerance with a huge, delicious, gluten-free chocolate doughnut for breakfast. Dave chose regular chocolate.

In the shade of the skyscrapers, it was crisply cold. Out in the open of Millennium Park, the sun shone down and I regretted having changed into my jeans. By day, we were taken aback by how friendly people were, from strangers offering to take our photo at the official Route 66 start sign, to the will.i.am lookalike who photobombed us outside the famous Chicago Theatre. But at night, we felt much less safe. Shady characters hung around street corners, making us uneasy as twilight fell.

We'd landed in the US the previous afternoon and joined the long queue at border control. Almost two hours later – an average wait from experience, so be prepared – we set off to pick up our rental vehicle. Although we'd hoped on reserving a traditional American muscle car, our travel agent had only been able to book a 'full-size' option in advance, so we were keen to see if we could upgrade. After being told there was just one sports car left – a Dodge Challenger in my favourite colour (red) – we quickly handed over the extra cash and set off for the bright lights of the city.

This is where we made, perhaps, the first poor decision of our trip. It turns out Chicago car parks are expensive (comparable to central London). But, if we'd picked up a car in the city centre rather than the airport, we would have needed to organise alternative transport to our hotel. And that sought-after muscle car may not have been available (we were advised that O'Hare had a better selection of cars than downtown). This is something to consider before you book.

After recovering from spending more than a motel room on a parking space, we checked into a little piece of American history. The Palmer House Hilton (17 E Monroe St) originally opened in 1871, but it burned down 13 days later during the Great Chicago Fire. Rather than admit defeat, its owner, Chicago businessman Potter Palmer, set to work rebuilding the hotel and reopened it in 1873. Today, this exquisitely grand building, with its golden-clad elevators, chandeliers and ornate features, is America's longest continually operating hotel. And it's stunning. A walk through its illuminated doorway, through the marble-covered lobby and up the stairs to the dimly lit, but (importantly) well-stocked, Potter's Bar made me feel like a movie star. We weren't quite lucky enough to stay in one of the hotel's elaborate suites, but our room, complete with mahogany chest of drawers and a velvet dressed armchair, was still enormous – there were two double beds!

Following a brief meal (during which we could barely keep our eyes open) and a good night's sleep to fight off the jet-lag, we set off early the next day for our first stint of sightseeing. With just two full days in Chicago, our itinerary prioritised the city's most iconic, but central, landmarks, alongside Route 66 attractions. Unfortunately, we didn't have time to seek out a speakeasy and the Cubs weren't playing baseball during our stay.

We started with a building that was once the tallest in the world. Standing at 110 storeys and 1,450 feet, Chicago's Willis Tower (233 S Wacker Dr.) was designed to house retail giant Sears Roebuck and Company in the early 1970s. The city's most famous landmark took just three years to build, using enough concrete to make an eight-lane, five-mile-long highway. Originally known as the Sears Tower, the building was renamed in 2009 when global insurance broker Willis Group Holdings gained the naming rights as part of a leasing deal. The decision remains controversial to this day, with some Chicagoans refusing to call it by its new title.

The Willis Tower's main attraction is 'The Ledge' – a glass-bottomed balcony extending 4.3 feet from the edge of the building's Skydeck viewing platform, at 1,353 feet in the air. Each day, hundreds of eager tourists take the elevator up 103 floors in just over 60 seconds to see some of the best views the city has to offer.

Stepping out onto The Ledge is an unforgettable experience. Holding firmly onto the edge of the glass box, I slowly walked out into the centre of the transparent floor and looked down at Chicago below. The cars, the people, the sidewalks and the long, wide roads all looked so tiny such a long way down. High up, I felt exposed; there were just a few reinforced sheets of glass protecting me from falling to my death. Dave was much braver and walked straight out into the middle of the box, before sitting down to pose for a photo! When a couple of daredevils began jumping up and down, I decided it was time to leave.

If a glass-bottomed balcony isn't your thing (I don't think it was mine), the Skydeck still provides some stunning views of the Chicago skyline. Large windows surround the room, offering fantastic photo opportunities, without the need to step out onto The Ledge. The experience also includes an insightful short film, providing a useful overview of the tower's history, a number of interactive quizzes (which are fun to play whilst you queue for the lift) and a chance to visit the sizable gift shop. Dave and I had perhaps a little bit too much fun there trying on novelty hot dog hats, but the shop is also good for a Chicago souvenir or two. Arrive early and on a weekday to try and beat the queues – we had a 1.5-hour wait before we could enter the lift, despite arriving shortly after the attraction opened.

The Willis Tower may be Chicago's most famous building, but Millennium Park is its most celebrated outdoor retreat. With so much to look at, it's easy to see why. And it's free, so one to prioritise if you're on a budget. Located on East Randolph Street, the park marks an abrupt, but welcome, change in the downtown landscape. Across the road, the city's network of skyscrapers are a maze. They stand so high that they cast continual shadows over the sidewalks, making a stroll through the shopping and entertainment district an often chilly experience (so pack a jumper).

But when you reach North Michigan Avenue, the city opens up, and you can feel the sun on your skin for the first time. There are no more concentrations of skyscrapers. Simply flat parkland, bicycle tracks and footpaths leading to the waterfront, with Lake Michigan stretching as far as the eye can see. It's so vast that the lake looks like the ocean.

The stark contrast between high-rise buildings and vast open spaces is a key aspect of Chicago's urban design. Although Millennium Park opened in 2004 (four years after it was supposed to), intentions to extend the city's parkland began as far back as 1909, when architect Daniel Burnham published his Plan of Chicago. Co-authored by Edward H. Bennett, the document set out plans to improve the fast-expanding metropolis by reshaping Chicago's central area. Although the plan also suggested widening streets and developing a new railroad, you'll soon see that his changes to the lakefront had the biggest impact on the city. Burnham wanted to reclaim this area for the people of Chicago and devised plans to extend the parks along the water's edge. Today, as much as 25 miles of the city's 29-mile-long lakefront is designated as public parkland. And it's enchanting.

Millennium Park, conceived in 1997 as a project to mark the start of the 21st century, is a 24.5-acre collection of art, well-kept lawns, beautiful gardens, coffee shops and even an open-air theatre. At its heart sits Cloud Gate, or 'The Bean' as locals lovingly call it. This 100-ton stainless steel sculpture, designed by British artist Sir Anish Kapoor, provides some stunning photo opportunities. Its curved surface (shaped like a coffee bean) reflects the Chicago skyline, offering a completely different perspective from every angle you look. As I'm sure you will, Dave and I had great fun taking selfies of our reflections; Cloud Gate contributed to some of the most artistic shots of our trip.

Just past The Bean is another of Chicago's must-see attractions: Crown Fountain. The water feature is constructed of two glass 50-foot towers, each using thousands of LED lights to display video footage of the faces of volunteer Chicagoans. But watch out – at the end of each five-minute video, water sprays out of the mouth on screen. You've been warned! During our visit, children played in its puddles, dodging the water as it squirted from electronic lips. The fountain is a charming example of Chicago community spirit and of how art is always more fun when it's interactive and designed to unite people.

Beyond Millennium Park, you should stop by Navy Pier to savour an ice cream whilst watching the jet-skiers bounce across Lake Michigan. Free to enter, the pier boasts a fantastic collection of fairground games, amusements, restaurants and live entertainment, stretching out onto the water. Its central attraction is (now) the 196-foot-high Centennial Wheel. The ride is a replacement of the 148-foot version we enjoyed during our trip (we felt the breeze on our faces in open-air carriages, but today's offering is more akin to the London Eye). You'll still witness some fantastic views and get a chance to experience an important part of the city's history – the Centennial Wheel is located on the site of the world's first-ever Ferris wheel, created for the 1893 World's Columbian Exposition.

Also known as Chicago's World Fair, the event was another of Daniel Burnham's contributions to Chicago's architecture and gave rise to its infamous nickname – the 'Windy City'. You may hear more about how the place came to bear this affectionate moniker aboard a boat tour of the Chicago River – one of the best ways to view the skyscrapers whilst taking in a history lesson. Surprisingly, the name has little to do with the weather blowing in from Lake Michigan, but actually refers to two important events in the late 19th century.

Between 8 and 10 October 1871, the Great Chicago Fire killed an estimated 300 people and caused approximately $200 million worth of damage (equivalent to nearly $4 billion, or £2.8 billion, today). The blaze destroyed an area four miles long and almost a mile wide, crippling buildings and homes, which were predominately made from wood at the time. Even the river was engulfed in flames. For 126 years, urban legend told how the fire began at the home of Patrick and Catherine O'Leary when the pair's cow kicked over a lantern. It took until 1997 for the cow to be proclaimed innocent by the Chicago City Council, following an hour-long hearing using new historical evidence. To this day, the true cause of the blaze is unknown.

In the years that followed, Chicago was rebuilt to far exceed its former glory (it's probably my favourite American city). In the 1890s, officials set about planning to show the globe that the city had risen from the ashes of the Great Fire by bidding for the World Fair. It was a battle fraught with contention. New York, St Louis and Washington DC were amongst the competition, all vying for the privilege of hosting an event that would gain mass attention. It seemed Chicago was punching above its weight. *The New York Sun* claimed the city's politicians were 'full of hot air'; Chicago couldn't build such an important exposition even if it did win. And the Windy City name was born. In 1893, Daniel Burnham and Fredrick Law Olmsted proved the critics wrong, opening the exhibition as a prototype of what they considered a city should be like. But the Windy City nickname has stuck.

Although a river tour is well worth the investment in time and cash (try Wendella Boats at 400 N Michigan Ave), it's not a substitute for a walk around the city's magnificent architecture. By far the highlight of our time spent in Chicago was a trip to the Tribune Tower, the home of the *Chicago Tribune* newspaper. Its beautiful neo-Gothic design, with stunning vertical strips of limestone and glass, topped by a crown of detailed buttresses, was the result of a competition to create the world's most beautiful office building (and it really is, in my opinion). But it's the output of another of the building's competitions that Dave and I had a lot of fun discovering.

Editor of the *Chicago Tribune*, Robert McCormick was a war correspondent. Whilst travelling around Europe during the First World War, he had somehow managed to collect pieces of historic buildings. Inspired by his finds, McCormick challenged the paper's travelling reporters to continue his endeavours and bring back chunks of other famous structures to insert into the outer façade of the paper's HQ. Walking around the building, you can glimpse chunks of the Great Pyramid, the Great Wall of China, Edinburgh Castle and even an entire façade from the Houses of Parliament. Selfies and photos pointing at the various chunks of embedded rock are obligatory, or at least they were for us.

The building also features fragments of relics you'll see elsewhere on your Route 66 journey – the Lincoln Tomb and rock from Arizona's Petrified Forest (which signs throughout the park command visitors to not remove). Although built a few years before Route 66, in many ways the Tribune Tower embodies the very things that make the road such a joy to encounter. It combines beautiful architecture with the absolute absurd. And it does so magnificently.

* * * *

Breakfast at Lou Mitchell's, Chicago, has long been considered the official way to start any westbound trip along the Mother Road. At 565 West Jackson Boulevard, it sits on Route 66's original starting point, before this street became one-way (eastbound) in the 1950s. Nowadays the start sign (a must-see photo point for any Route 66 adventurer) can be found on Adams Street, which is where US 66 begins today.

Sitting in one of the restaurant's vintage booths, we got our first taste of retro Americana and an important US dining custom – all-you-can-drink coffee. As soon as our mugs were emptied, a waitress was on standby to refill them with steaming black liquid. I'm a tea-drinker, so the never-ending supply of coffee was a little overwhelming. But by the time we'd visited a few more diners, we'd devised a coping strategy that I'll happily share with you; always leave some of your beverage still in the cup (it's not just coffee that all-you-can-drink applies to).

I dread to think of the amount of food and drink wasted in the US. But you cannot fault American hospitality, and the staff at Lou Mitchells are the perfect example of it. Nothing was too much trouble. Not even my gluten-free chocolate-chip pancakes, which were stacked high and covered in ripe strawberries. Our waitress was friendly, funny and made us feel incredibly welcome. The people of Route 66 are one of the road's greatest assets.

Getting out of Chicago was not such an enjoyable experience for two Brits in a bright red Dodge adjusting to the American Highway Code. The roads were complicated, and we needed complete concentration not to miss the several junctions and turns. Not least because the police seemed to be closing streets at every corner for what later turned out to be a TV commercial shoot. The *EZ66 Guide*, although initially difficult to follow, proved invaluable, and we eventually arrived safely at our first stop – Wilmington, home of the Launching Pad Drive-In.

Having only just eaten, it wasn't food we were looking for at the Launching Pad. We were here seeking another quirk of the Will Rogers Highway, the Gemini Giant. At 30 feet tall, this fibreglass spaceman stands in the parking lot, holding a rocket which bears the diner's name. He's one of several 'Muffler Men' (given the name because they used to hold exhaust pipes, or mufflers as they are called in the US) and many other seemingly random oversized sculptures that stand proudly on the Route 66 roadside. But these giants aren't perhaps as obscure as they first seem.

With a wealth of restaurants, motels and tourist

attractions competing for travellers' attention all along the 2,448-mile road trip, these colossal structures form a key part of many establishments' marketing strategies. Owners erect the giants in the hope of tempting families out of their cars and into their businesses to spend their hard-earned cash. For many years, no amount of novelty fibreglass could turn around the Launching Pad's fortune, though – the restaurant was closed and up for sale during our visit. However, things look set to change; at the time of writing, the diner has secured new owners and will soon be refurbished!

For fans of the kitsch and slightly ridiculous, the Gemini Giant is a great deal of fun. He makes a wonderful prop for any camera-wielding tourist looking to take a few comedy shots of their friends and family. He was also the site of our first extraordinary Route 66 experience.

When travelling in a pair, taking photographs as a couple can be difficult, especially when a 30-foot spaceman makes it near-on impossible to get the right angle for a selfie. Luckily, one of the young lads waiting in line for his turn to take a few snaps volunteered to take the picture for us, so Dave and I could both be in shot. Upon hearing his British accent, we asked where he was from. James said he lived in Leeds, but he was born in Braintree, Essex – the town I grew up in. It seemed we'd lived in the same place for years, but it had taken a nine-hour plane trip and the appeal of the world's ultimate road trip for us to meet. Such is the wonder and draw of Route 66.

Upon leaving Wilmington, we continued to Pontiac, making a few unscheduled stops along the way. No matter how much planning has gone into your trip, you'll still find things on the drive that you didn't know existed. It's the charm of finding these unexpected delights that's part of the fun and adventure of travelling the US by car. Dwight was home to the first of these additions to our itinerary – as the temptation of seeing Route 66's longest continually serving gas station was too much to drive past.

A former Texaco garage, Ambler's (W. Waupansie St) was exactly the type of postcard perfect Route 66 relic we'd hoped to find on our trip. The station is complete with a white wooden-cladded exterior and beautiful red vintage gas pumps, making the perfect backdrop for photos of our Dodge (even if it was a more modern vehicle than those of the road's heyday). The garage is now a tourist information spot, run by volunteers from the village. Two retirees showed us around and asked us to add a pin to their wall map, marking the hometown of every visitor to the station that year. There were pins as widespread as Australia, Iraq and Russia.

After visiting another beautifully restored gas station in Odell, we pulled into Pontiac – my favourite stop so far. A stroll around the city's downtown reveals several painted fibreglass cars (sadly 1957 Chevys and pick-up trucks rather than actual Pontiacs) and more than 20 beautiful murals depicting Pontiac's past. These make for some fantastic photos (yes, it is possible for a grown woman to fit in a miniature Chevy), especially the large Route 66 shield on the rear of the Illinois Route 66 Hall of Fame and Museum (free entry).

Parked just along from the painting is a legend of America's Main Street – a converted school bus camper belonging to the late Bob Waldmire. Waldmire was somewhat of a Route 66 celeb and the inspiration for Fillmore in *Cars*. He travelled the highway in the yellow bus, which he termed his 'Mobile Route 66 Information Center', collecting memorabilia and selling intricate hand-drawn postcards depicting his favourite destinations along the road. The sketches on them are so detailed that we used them at our wedding reception as a novel take on a guest book; we asked people to leave us messages on the back of the postcards and insert them into our custom-painted US mailbox.

Waldmire's lifelong obsession with Route 66 was spawned by a road trip with his parents when he was a boy, resulting in the most eccentric travelling home I've ever laid eyes on. Imagine if someone took a static caravan, covered it in wood so it looked a bit like an arc, chopped it in half and stuck it on top of a yellow school bus. It has to be seen to be believed.

* * * *

For Dave and me, the decision to travel Route 66 was as much a result of my overwhelming desire to indulge in 1950s nostalgia as our combined appetite for adventure. I was looking for lessons on the art and culture of the past, but I didn't expect to learn so much about the American culture of today – something that expressed itself differently in every state we visited. A perfect example of this occurred during our stay at the Route 66 Hotel and Conference Centre, Springfield (625 E St Joseph St).

Originally erected as the Mother Road's first Holiday Inn, the hotel is now locally owned and operated. As its name suggests, the establishment has embraced its 66 history; it serves as a mini museum, complete with classic vehicles in the lobby and an array of signage and other memorabilia from the road scattered over its walls and ceilings (including half a drag car shell, which Dave – who races cars and runs a motorsport company – took particular delight in seeing). After grabbing a bite to eat in the inn's retro-themed diner, we headed to the bar for a nightcap.

We were soon joined by an American bridge engineer who was relaxing after a long day spent repairing a nearby freeway. Intrigued by our accents, he asked where we were from and what we were doing in Springfield. After correcting his initial suspicion that we were from Australia (it always makes me laugh how the Essex accent is interpreted abroad – he wasn't the first person on our trip to think we were from Down Under), we explained we were on holiday. 'Vacation,' he said. 'I've heard people use that word. It's not something I've experienced myself.' He must have been in his fifties.

He told us he worked mostly outside on the roads for six days a week, four hours away from his wife, who lived in the next state. Although workers can stay in cabins on the construction sites, he chose to stay in the hotel because it's more comfortable. He often shared a room with his colleague and, although many lodgings offer discounts for construction workers, his half of the bill was paid for out of his own pocket. On Sundays, he would travel home to see his wife and cut the grass.

The world's media can sometimes give the United States a bad reputation. But that evening in Springfield showed me something wonderful about today's Americans. Even though the bridge engineer could only afford to see his family for a few hours each week and spent most of his spare cash on the luxury of a warm bed, he insisted on buying us a beer. We were the ones with the money to travel the breadth of his country, with dollars reserved for sightseeing, but when we offered to pay, he wouldn't accept. When Dave tried to return the favour, he insisted on buying us another. 'American hospitality,' he called it. It was the same kindness, community spirit and appreciation of our tourism that we felt in every state we visited. UK newspapers may report on questionable US politics, but the real America is all heart.

We woke the next morning to heavy rain and severe weather warnings. It seemed towns all along I-40 – the Route 66 corridor – were on alert for storms and flash flooding. I spent the drive into downtown looking out the window at blackened skies, hoping not to spot a triangular-shaped whirling cloud on our way to Springfield (as well as a planner, I'm also a worrier!).

It may not be home to the Simpsons, (that title is

reserved for Oregon, according to Matt Groening) but Springfield, Illinois was once the home of President Abraham Lincoln. The Abraham Lincoln Presidential Library and Museum was therefore a must (112 N 6th St) and it should be for you too. The museum is more akin to a small theme park than the traditional exhibition and explanation you'd find in Britain, and it's absolutely wonderful. Live shows, with smoke machines and real actors are just some of the devices used to tell the tale of Lincoln's rise to power, the Civil War and his assignation.

Our explorations in American history continued with a visit to the Lincoln Home National Historic Site (413 S 8th St), the place he lived with his family when it was announced he was elected to the House of Representatives. Much of the original furniture is still there (although I hope the outside toilet is a replica), so it's well worth booking a place on a free tour. These can be reserved from the Lincoln Home Visitor Center and are offered on a first-come-first-served basis. A short drive away is the Lincoln Tomb (1500 Monument Ave), where we visited the former president's spectacular burial place (make sure you go into the interior rooms) before heading to the Cozy Dog Drive In to sample the famed hot dog on a stick (and what we found to be some delicious skin-on fries). The Cozy Dog (2935 S 6th St) is a Route 66 landmark, home to the birthplace of the corn dog and owned by the family of the legendry Bob Waldmire (of Pontiac fame).

Our last stop in Springfield was a quick photo with Illinois' final giant, The Lauterbach (1569 Wabash Ave), which stands on the forecourt of a tyre garage. Despite being decapitated during a tornado in 2006, the giant's head is now firmly in place and boasts a fine beard and set of sideburns that rival my husband's. At nearly 20 feet tall, you can't miss him, but if you're concerned, look out for the huge American flag in his hand and his name clearly written down his leg.

The end stretch of Illinois 66 should be an absolute joy to drive. It combines the picturesque scenery of wide open fields and winding roads with unique features of the highway's history, including 1.4 miles of rare brick road dating from 1931. But with hammering rain and jet black skies, my melodramatic mind could only imagine a scene from Twister. Surely we'd soon have to leave the Dodge and seek shelter in one of the many abandoned barns, tying ourselves to a metal pipe with our belts in the hope we didn't fly away. We didn't see one car as we drove along the grass-lined tracks, and there didn't seem to be any signs of civilisation for miles. When we made it through, we took shelter in a fast food restaurant (right next to a tornado siren) to wait out the rain. According to the girls behind the counter, we were experiencing just another average Illinois storm! I guess it's true what they say about the Brits and their obsession with weather.

Despite my impending fear of doom, we did manage to enjoy one of the Illinois stretch's most obscure 'attractions' before we checked into our motel in Pontoon Beach. The 'Turkey Tracks' are just that, literally the marks of turkey feet in the road, made when the 1920s concrete was drying. They've been painted around and there's even a sign to mark their presence. Don't miss them!

4
THERE'S NO PLACE LIKE KANSAS, BUT MISSOURI'S GOOD TOO

Known as 'America's gateway to the west', St Louis is the first city you'll visit in Missouri. It's also a place where you can take a trip inside an egg.

Squashed into a tiny, white oval smaller than a double bed, the egg-shaped tram will take you to the top of one of St Louis' most famous landmarks, the Gateway Arch. It's not the smoothest of rides, especially for a couple with an average height of six foot, like Dave and me.

At 630 feet high, this stainless steel curve commemorates the cowboys' advancement into the Wild West in the 1800s. After a novel, albeit claustrophobic, journey to the viewing platform, you are treated to fantastic views across the metropolis and the mighty Mississippi River. On a clear day, you can see up to 30 miles in each direction, so it's well worth the bizarre three-minute ride to the top.

At the bottom of the Gateway Arch sits the Museum of Westward Expansion (which does exactly what it says on the tin). But I found the Old Courthouse opposite, a former slave auction, much more interesting.

In 1850, a judge here ruled that slave Dred Scott was a free man. He agreed with Scott's argument that a slave who had lived in a free state would, by Missouri law, remain free should he be taken back to the state by his master. Since Scott and his wife had lived in 'free' states for several years before returning to Missouri, legally they must have their freedom.

But slave masters weren't fans of losing. Scott's previous 'owner', Irene Emerson, successfully appealed the decision in 1852, kick-starting a series of court battles as the African American tried to reclaim his freedom.

In 1857, the United States Supreme Court dealt the final devastating blow. At the time, the US Constitution held that, regardless of whether they were slaves or free, Africans living in America were not citizens of the United States. Thus they could not claim citizenship or their freedom, so the case could not stand. Like all slaves in America, Scott was property. Just like that, all former slaves living in northern 'free states' no longer had their liberty.

In intensifying the ongoing slavery debate, the Dred Scott case is believed to be one of the key factors leading to the start of the American Civil War. But, despite its historical significance, the Old Courthouse (the place where the legal battle started) is only given fleeting mentions in the guidebooks we studied before our trip. It's a must-see landmark in our opinion. The place provides the chance to reflect on the horrors of slavery and emphasises exactly why human rights are worth fighting for. You can tour the courtrooms and read about the Dred Scott case, as well as historic slavery in the US more generally, in a number of exhibitions. The Old Courthouse is now also the visitor's centre for the Gateway Arch, so you can buy your timed ticket here to ride the egg tram.

After a reminder of how cruel human beings can be, you'll likely need an injection of happiness. And what better joy than ice cream? Or in this case, 'frozen custard'.

At 6726 Chippewa, Ted Drewes is a St Louis icon famous for its 'concretes' (ice cream in a tub to you and me). Customer service here, like almost everywhere on Route 66, is second to none. The shop's vast array of flavours range from the Dutchman (chocolate, butterscotch and pecan) to Cardinal Sin (complete with tart cherries and hot fudge) and Southern Delight (praline, pecans and butterscotch), to name just a few. Don't worry, the servers will spend some time running through them all with you – they take great pride in helping customers make their perfect selection.

Despite being tempted by Terramizzou (chocolate and pistachio), Dave and I both went for classic vanilla to experience a concrete in its purest form. Our desserts were passed through the serving window in neon yellow cups, along with a memento bumper sticker. Thinking of our rental deposit, we decided not to affix it to our hired Dodge and drove on to our next stop, Cuba.

* * * *

Despite its name, this particular Cuba has little to do with the famous missile crisis. But the small town is the site of the legendary Wagon Wheel Motel, and thus is every bit as exciting as a trip to the Caribbean island. At least for a Route 66 explorer, I imagine.

We'd been told to watch out for the abundance of 'Meramec Caverns' billboards along the way (the family attraction is rumoured to have been a Jesse James hideout). The signs didn't disappoint – they were painted onto the roofs of barns almost every five minutes along the road. The caverns themselves are actually in Stanton (1135 Highway W) where you can take guided tours through the caves (ending with a patriotic light show), ride a riverboat and even slide along a zip wire. We couldn't fit a visit into our trip, but it's on our itinerary for next time.

As for the Wagon Wheel, (901 E Washington St), with its original neon sign, the motel is an even bigger treat for the eyes. Lovingly restored cabins are grouped on the lawn, with space to park right outside each door. Our room consisted of a bed, table and chairs, TV and sink in the main living area, then a cute toilet and shower room. It was a shame it was cold on the night of our stay because it would have been lovely to sit outside next to the fire pit, underneath the tree with a hanging chandelier. Instead, we walked next door to the Missouri Hicks BBQ and feasted on pulled pork with our choice of seven different sauces. At night, we were sung to sleep by the horns of freight trains and the whistles of crickets – if you're not into the sounds of the Wild West, you might want to bring earplugs! But don't let that put you off. The Wagon Wheel is one of the route's most famous lodgings, so you need to book ahead.

Named Missouri's 'Mural City', the wall paintings along Cuba's streets are one of the town's delights, along with its retro Phillips 66 gas station (now The FourWay restaurant – 102 W Washington Blvd). Intrigued by the town, we decided to find out more about it in the Crawford County Historical Society and Museum (308 N Smith St) and highly recommend that you do too. Inside we had the good fortune of meeting a wonderful tour guide who had lived her entire life on a farm just outside of the town. The small museum is housed in her old high school and is filled with photographs and relics from the Route 66 heyday.

As we walked through the displays, we saw old school uniforms and a replica classroom, with 1930s maps, desks and textbooks. The stairs were lined with the wedding dresses of the town's women, including our guide's own special gown, along with military uniforms donated by the men of Cuba and other artefacts from the First World War and the Civil War. Whilst we took in the exhibits, our guide recounted charming stories of Route 66 life, including tales of how she and her friends had to use underground tunnels to get to class because the road was so busy when she was young. Now you can walk across it with ease. Although the museum's three floors can be toured in less than an hour, we could have spent many more there listening to her, but it was time to get back on the road and head to Fanning – to take a photo at the world's (now second) largest rocking chair.

The oversized piece of furniture is another of Route 66's stunts, designed to pull passing punters off the road and into roadside attractions, in this case the Fanning 66 Outpost (5957 Highway Zz). At 42 feet four inches tall and 27,500 pounds, the 'Rocker' is rumoured to have been built by a man without an engineering qualification – so it may be just as well that it doesn't actually rock. Just a year after we visited, the beast was stripped of its title when an even bigger chair was constructed in Illinois, causing its owners to paint the original monument bright red and rename it 'The Route 66 Red Rocker'. But size isn't everything, as they say, so don't let the chair's second-place status deter you. Despite regarding ourselves as tall, Dave and I were dwarfed by the Rocker, making for some humorous photos. Plus, it was nice to imagine what it might feel like to be a Borrower for the day. Stop by the store too – they sell homemade popcorn and fudge!

* * * *

Next on our agenda was another town with the same name as a country, this time called 'Lebanon'. But on our way there, we had to make an unexpected stop. As we drove on towards the Devils [sic] Elbow Bridge, we heard laughter and shouting coming from a wooden-clad bar. Rows of Harley-Davidsons stood along the outer wall of the Elbow Inn Bar & Tavern (21050 Teardrop Rd), and I had the distinct fear that we might have accidentally stumbled across a Hells Angel's hangout.

Dave, on the other hand, was simply intrigued and set about searching for the entrance. Gingerly, we opened it and were met by several bikers in leather jackets and chaps, who immediately stopped talking and stared at us. Before I had time to worry that my worst fears had been confirmed, the bikers gave us the warmest welcome. We sat drinking with them for what felt like hours, listening to tales of '100-Mile Mike', who travelled the country writing about Harleys, and admiring the unique decor – bras hung from the ceiling, donated by visitors. I decided to keep mine firmly in place!

Devastatingly, Devils Elbow was hit by severe flooding in May 2017, which destroyed homes and flowed straight through the Elbow Inn. Thanks to the hard work of the town's community, and donations from Route 66 fans across the world, the bar reopened a few months later – minus the ladies' undergarments. The staff and patrons are just as friendly as ever, though, so drop in for a pit stop and grab a bite to eat.

That night, we checked into room 24 of Lebanon's legendary Munger Moss Motel (1336 Route 66), complete with original neon sign. Photos of past road stops, motels and attractions covered almost every inch of the walls. A mustard yellow reading chair channelled 1950s glamour, along with the maroon and gold bedspread with tasselled cushion. Although a little over the top with its stripy wallpaper, the small bathroom was really quite quaint, complete with delicate net curtain, hiding the pink tiled shower, and an ornate white and gold oval mirror next to a stack of fluffy white towels. Each Route-66-themed room is unique and styled by the owner, Ramona, so be sure to reserve well in advance.

After unpacking, I couldn't resist the temptation to try a local delicacy – southern-fried catfish. Drowd's Catfish BBQ (1760 W Elm St) has won awards for the hand-breaded stuff (my wheat intolerance took some abuse in small-town USA)! Dinners are served with hush puppies (fried tubes of cornmeal batter) and a choice of three sides from a huge list, including everything from fried okra (only available after 4 p.m., apparently) to baked potato, and cottage cheese to cabbage. There were all-you-can-eat options too, but I settled on just three pieces coated in lemon pepper with all the trimmings. Dave opted for a burger – if catfish is a little too off the wall for you, the restaurant also has a sizable selection of BBQ food. The hickory smoked plates looked amazing!

After a delicious meal, we spent the evening at the Starlite Lanes bowling alley (1331 Route 66) across from the Munger Moss – and then later drinking and chatting until the early hours. We were joined by Lyn and Mike, two Australian roadies we met earlier in the day at Mr C's Trading Post, just up the road from the motel. The shop has since been put up for sale after the sad passing of Mr C, creator of Route 66 Soda. We were lucky to have the pleasure of meeting him, and we'll always treasure the conversations we shared that afternoon. As for Lyn and Mike, we still chat to them online. You'll make lots of friends on Route 66.

* * * *

Following a quick, but tasty, breakfast at Faye's Diner (691 W Elm St – try the omelettes), where we were met with a bunch of *Duck Dynasty* fans on their way hunting, it was on to the Gay Parita Sinclair Station (21118 Old 66, Ash Grove). As soon as we got out of our car, owner Gary Turner was at the gate to ask us if we'd like a cup of coffee and a doughnut, on the house of course. We looked around his replica gas station, built by Gary himself and complete with vintage cars and road signs, and then had a seat on his front porch to talk about the Will Rogers Highway. Soon we were joined by two other tourists, who pulled up in their blue Mustang. When we asked where they were from, we couldn't believe one was from Chelmsford, half an hour from our hometown.

It soon became apparent that Gary was a Route 66 legend. He knew almost everything there is to know about America's Main Street and we revelled in listening to his stories about the route and the friends he'd made over the years. He introduced us to his wife Lena and joked about how she beats him with her walking stick (she really was joking!). It wasn't long afterwards that she knocked her stick over, right onto Dave's knee, and we all fell about laughing because she was now attacking visitors as well as her husband! Gary showed us pictures of attractions we must explore on our journey and insisted we visit his friend Dan's gift shop on Santa Monica Pier when we reached the end in LA (we kept our promise). After a picture with Gary and his Route 66 flag, a ritual for any guest who stops by, we bid farewell to them both and began our journey towards Kansas.

A few months after we returned from America, Facebook brought us news that Gary had passed away. Shortly afterwards, Lena passed too. Although we'd only known them for that one afternoon, their passing shocked us as if they'd been close friends. The warmth and passion for Route 66 they showed us that day will stay with us forever, and we talk about that experience frequently. Gary prided himself on making 'friends for life' at his gas station, and that's exactly what we became that afternoon. As a tribute, we dedicated a tier of our wedding cake to his and Lena's memory by painting the Gay Parita onto its side.

I'm sorry that you won't have the pleasure of meeting Gary and Lena, but I hope you'll still stop by to meet their successor. Nicknamed 'Little Gary', Barbara Barnes-Turner, their daughter, has revived the garage and is committed to safeguarding her parents' legacy so future generations can enjoy gorgeous Americana and make more lifelong friendships. I hope you leave with the fondest of memories, just like we did.

* * * *

If you're looking to save time on your American adventure, you might be considering avoiding Kansas altogether. As the only Route 66 state to be completely bypassed by the interstate, you might think you'd be forgiven for driving straight past it. But you'd only be cheating yourself. What you might gain in real time, you'd most certainly lose in time well spent.

At only 13 miles long, what the Kansas Mother Road may lack in size, it certainly makes up for with an unmissable attraction. Standing at the top of Main Street Galena, 'Cars on the Route' is a renovated Kan-O-Tex service station turned cafe, famous for an old rusty truck. Named 'Tow Tater', this pick-up is rather special. He's instantly recognisable to Disney fans as the inspiration behind Tow Mater, Lightning McQueen's best buddy in *Cars*.

Melba the Mouth told us all about how Tow Tater became an international movie star. Don't worry, it's a nickname the cafe's founder relishes. By her own admission, Melba talks fast, loudly and excessively. It was nice to meet someone who loves a natter as much as me! Melba inherited Tow Tater when she and three friends bought the former Little's Service Station with the intention of renovating it and putting Kansas back on the Route 66 map. Tow Tater had a tree growing right through his middle, so Melba and her pals – the '4 Women on the Route' (as the cafe was named then) – decided to cut their losses and sell him.

Little did they know then that Route 66 historian, Michael Wallis, had travelled the route through Kansas six years earlier on a Pixar research trip for a new animated film. When his party reached Galena, animator Joe Ranft spotted the old rusty vehicle and soon became inspired. Tow Mater was born.

Wallis travelled through Galena again after the movie's release and was surprised to find the pickup had gone. When Melba realised what had happened, she was mortified and committed to help Michael find the truck. Luckily the pair weren't disappointed; the original Tow Tater now stands outside the building alongside a reconstruction of Disney's Mater and Red the fire truck. All three have cartoon eyes, so bring your cameras.

Following the success of the film, the '4 Women on the Route' became 'Cars on the Route' and now serves food most days. We stopped for lunch and a chat with two of its proprietors, before heading over the road to another popular *Cars* attraction – a mural which can be seen during one of the film's most difficult scenes, when Mater informs Lightning he owes him $32,000 in legal fees.

Before leaving Kansas, we also stopped by a restored Phillips 66 gas station in the nearby town of Baxter Springs (940 Military Ave). With its red sloping roof mounted with chimney pots, the building could be mistaken for a cottage if it wasn't for the large garage door (and huge Phillips sign). But this particular 'look' is no accident. During the Great Depression, stalling demand and surplus supply sent oil prices tumbling and gas stations into administration. Those that survived needed to find inventive ways to acquire and retain customers. In the uncertainty of the economic climate, many created these cottage-like buildings in the hope of associating their brand with safety and security – homes from homes to refuel and relax out on the open road. Today, you'll find a visitor's centre and a great spot for a photo, so stop and get snapping.

They say the best things come in small packages, and that's certainly true of Route 66 in the Sunflower State.

Make sure you don't cut Kansas out of your trip.

5
I'D SOONER BE IN OKLAHOMA

I've never been one for celebrities. My favourite success stories have always been about the ordinary people who do extraordinary things. So when I read about the Sooner State's Andy Payne, the 20-year-old high school graduate who ran – and won – a 3,423.5 mile race across Route 66, I claimed myself another everyday hero. And I knew we had to visit his hometown – Foyil, Oklahoma.

Part Cherokee, Andy entered the 1928 International Trans-Continental Foot Race (perhaps accurately nicknamed the 'Bunion Derby') faced with dwindling employment prospects. His family farm was struggling (as many were in the pre-Dust Bowl era), so he entered the race to win its $25,000 prize (worth more than $360,000, or more than £250,000, in 2018), pay off his family's mortgage and marry his girlfriend. The race began in LA and ended in New York City and was organised by Oklahoma business man, and 'Father of Route 66', Cyrus Avery. Taking in much of America's Main Street, the race was a stunt to promote the newly created highway.

Andy ran five miles to school every day and was a regular on his high school track, but he was still unknown on the professional running scene. When he went to secure funding from the local chamber of commerce to cover his entry fees, the committee humoured him by coughing up $75 for his enthusiasm ($1,092, or £775, in 2018). His father borrowed the remainder. Before the race, not one reporter listed Andy as a potential winner – the odds were on Arthur F. H. Newton, from England, the current record holder for amateur running events up to 100 miles.

But that didn't put Andy off. He trained by running up to 30 miles each day, and on 4 March 1928, he joined the other 275 contestants at the start line. Over the following three months, entrants retired due to foot and leg injuries, severe weather and tooth infections. Some were even hit by road traffic. A few weeks into the race Andy developed tonsillitis, but still he kept running. By the final stage, only 55 entrants remained.

On 26 May 1928, Andy Payne – the amateur from Oklahoma – won the Bunion Derby with a 15-hour lead. The underdog became an overnight celebrity. He paid off the family mortgage, built a house, got married and retired from professional racing. He became the clerk of the Supreme Court of Oklahoma and kept the role for 38 years.

Just off Andy Payne Boulevard, past the Bunion Derby marker, stands a lone bronze statue of the runner with a plaque celebrating his achievement. Of all the Route 66 stories (and there are many), the tale of Andy Payne will always be my favourite. Standing there in front of such a simple monument and thinking of his extraordinary achievement, is a reminder that, with hard work, passion and determination, anyone can do just about anything. He's the epitome of the American Dream. And that's certainly worth a quick visit, don't you think?

But if David versus Goliath stories don't inspire you, maybe you'd enjoy another of Route 66's legendary oddities

– a 20-foot-tall blue whale.

Situated in Catoosa, the Blue Whale (2600 OK-66) roadside attraction was built as an anniversary present for the wife of retired resident Hugh S. Davis. The result is an 80-foot-long structure, which looks like it's covered in paper mache. For years locals picnicked by the whale and swam in the pond it sits on top of, jumping from its tail into the cool water. Nowadays, swimming is banned, but you can still visit the whale for a quick selfie and pop into the gift shop. I'm sure you'll have a whale of a time.

* * * *

America is not known for its fine cuisine, but if there is one culinary achievement that the United States should be celebrated for, it has to be its outstanding contribution to breakfast. And Tally's on Tulsa's Route 66 is a mighty fine example (11th and Yale). I tucked into chicken fried steak, which I must admit (again) wasn't wheat-free, but luckily it didn't affect me (if you are coeliac, there are non-gluten dishes available here, but check the menu to be sure). The Midwest classic actually has very little to do with poultry and is served with hash browns (forget the full English type, hash browns on Route 66 are just piles of fried potatoes). Regardless, it set me up for a drive into downtown Tulsa to visit the gorgeous Blue Dome District.

Now when I say 'gorgeous', please don't expect grassy side banks and flower-lined pavements. Think more Shoreditch, London or Manchester's Northern Quarter, in vibe. But if you love art deco architecture, like myself, you really will be in heaven. The area (between just before East 51st and East 54th) is named after a beautiful blue domed gas station, and its blocks are lined with an assortment of zigzag-style buildings with geometric roofs renovated into cafes, bars and shops. Of course, like any up-and-coming neighbourhood, there is still a lot of empty and dilapidated structures, but the overall effect is something quite stunning; modern-day Tulsa is very different to the boring, middle-of-nowhere place Chandler complained about in the TV show *Friends*. To Dave and me, the area is an emblem of Route 66 picking itself up and dusting itself off, redefining itself for the younger generation – the Blue Dome District is now famous for its arts and nightlife scene.

On the way out of the city, we paid a quick visit to Red Fork to see an enormous old train, which marks the importance of the railroad in the development of the US. On the same site is a disused oil derrick (also free to look at), signifying that Tulsa was once the oil capital of the world. This is a good place to stop for a photo (including next to the Tulsa 66 shield) and read the attraction's informative signage to get some useful context for the next stage of your journey; fossil fuel is something you'll be reminded of continually as you leave the metropolis and see field after field of oil derricks and pumps on the road to Oklahoma City.

As you head towards the state capital, the landscape opens up, and you truly get the sense you're in in the Wild West. The scenery is different in every Route 66 state (it's another of the joys of travelling America by road), and Oklahoma couldn't be a starker contrast to the regions you'll have driven through before it. The fields are covered with deep red soil, making it quite harrowing to imagine all of those houses covered in the stuff during the long years of the Dust Bowl.

Surrounded by all that soil is the first of the town of Arcadia's two unique attractions – The Round Barn (107 OK-66). The building takes its name from its shape – a complete circle. A marvel of farm architecture, the roadside attraction should be a must-see stop on your itinerary and is rumoured to be the most photographed place on Route 66. Nowadays the venue is mostly used for weddings and parties, but we were lucky enough to arrive on the second Sunday of the month when live music was being played by a guitarist. The barn has been recently restored and its upper floor is trailed in fairy lights. On the lower level, you should spend some time looking around the museum to discover the barn's history, filled with vintage farming equipment, old photos, maps and other Route 66 memorabilia. The entire barn is free to enter, so perhaps pay a visit to the gift shop and purchase a postcard or too – proceeds go towards the attraction's upkeep.

A few minutes down the road you'll be greeted by the sight of a giant neon cola bottle. It marks the site of Pops 66 Soda Ranch (660 W Hwy 66), a fizzy-drink lover's Mecca. Filled with 700 types of soda, Pops is insane. We stayed for lunch in the cafe – I tried a very sickly grapefruit soda and Dave had authentic Route 66 Root Beer, previously made at Mr C's Trading Post in Lebanon. I lost count of how many of these he drank on our trip, so they must have been good – you'll be able to try one as the company is still in operation despite Mr C's passing. Even if you don't have time to eat, be sure to stop by and look at pretty much every flavour of fizzy drink ever made!

* * * *

The National Cowboy and Western Heritage Museum in Oklahoma City (1700 NE 63rd Street) is another of those interactive museums the Americans love so much. You can have a lot of fun posing in the replica western town, complete with furniture gathered from along Route 66. I've never held up a bank before, and I definitely enjoyed locking Dave in the jail. The Native American artefacts are also beautiful to behold.

Another history lesson awaits at the Oklahoma City National Memorial (620 N Harvey Ave) – and it's completely devastating. Here, in the foundations of the former Alfred P. Murrah Federal Building, sit 168 vacant chairs. Each represents a life taken when Timothy McVeigh and Terry Nichols detonated a truck full of explosives at 9.02 a.m. on 19 April 1995. The chairs are arranged in nine rows, a row to symbolise each floor of the building destroyed in America's deadliest domestic terrorist attack – the Oklahoma City Bombing. Sixteen chairs are slightly smaller than the rest – there was a nursery on-site.

Across the reflective pond, designed to bring calmness and tranquillity to the families torn apart by the tragedy, stands the Survivor Tree. At more than 100 years old, it withstood the blast. Nearby, an inscription reads: 'The spirit of this city and this nation will not be defeated; our deeply rooted faith sustains us.'

So that evening, after reflecting on one of the most poignant tributes to tragedy we'd ever seen, we decided to embrace the tree's message. We chose to celebrate the beauty of our host city with a tour of its Route 66 relics. We started with rather large milk bottle (2426 N Classen Blvd), which took us more than an hour to find after my first slip-up navigating (I'm not sure how we missed it – it's located on top of a triangular building right in the middle of a road junction, but, in my defence, the building is quite small). It's next to a CVS Pharmacy if you're struggling to place it. However, the neon sign at the nearby Tower Theatre (23rd St) is stunning, and we should know given how many times we drove past it looking for that bottle of milk!

We ended the night with a horse and carriage ride around Bricktown, the city's entertainment area, to take in its urban architecture (Bright Star Carriages pick up from numerous locations here – check their website for details). An abundance of restaurants and bars are housed in funky repurposed warehouses and the Chickasaw Bricktown Ballpark is right in the centre of the neighbourhood, home to the Oklahoma City Dodgers baseball team. You can also cruise along the canal in a water taxi to take in a history tour whilst looking up at the building facades along the water's edge.

You'll find Oklahoma 'entertainment' of a different sort in the historic Stockyard City district. A visit to its National Stockyards may be one of the loudest, most surreal experiences you'll ever have in your life (open to the public on Mondays only). The auction master speaks so loud and fast that you might think he's speaking a made-up language. Just don't wave your arms or you may find yourself with an unplanned souvenir – in the form of a herd of cows. Before leaving, you can even sample the beef in the Cattleman's Steakhouse (1309 S Agnew Ave), Oklahoma City's longest continually operating restaurant, or look around Main Street's numerous shops, stocked with an array of western items, from Stetson hats to cowboy boots.

Beyond the city, you'd do well to visit the Route 66 Museum in Clinton (2229 W Gary Blvd) to learn more about the history of the road from its creation to demise and subsequent rebirth. Entry requires a small fee ($7 at the time of writing, just under £5), which is more than worth parting with considering the wealth of bite-sized and easily digestible information the museum imparts. The exhibits give a real sense of what it might have been like to travel the road in the 1930s to 1950s, with details of historic gas prices and the cost of running cars helping to set the scene. There's also a replica 1950s diner, plenty of restored classic cars and an abundance of Route 66 artefacts, from road signs to gas pumps. The museum's glass-brick front and retro-inspired neon make quite a visual impact upon pulling into the parking lot too.

The National Route 66 Museum in Elk City further along the Mother Road (you can't miss the giant 66 shield) may also be great to visit, but it was closed when we arrived late afternoon (check opening hours online). We still had the chance to walk through its grounds, complete with a replica frontier town, totem poles and huge kachina doll (carved dolls given to Hopi tribe children to teach them about spirits), so at least we got some good photos. However, the stretch of historic Portland concrete road between Clinton and Foss more than made up for missing out on the inside of the museum. This section features original curbs (a real 66 rarity nowadays), so you'll have lots to look at from your car window.

Our last stop in Oklahoma was the town of Erick, home to the legendary Sand Hills Curiosity Shop (144 3rd St) and the Mediocre Music Makers, Harley and Annabel Russell. We'd first heard about these eccentric, self-proclaimed 'rednecks' in a Route 66 documentary where we noticed a striking resemblance between the attraction's exterior, completely covered with road signs, and Lizzy's Curio Shop in *Cars*. After reading more about Harley's unique way of serenading visitors with his non-PC guitar renditions and his shop's mad collection of antiques (none of which are actually for sale), we had to experience the place for ourselves. Sadly, at our time of visiting, it was closed due to Annabel's ongoing fight with cancer. The day after we landed back in the UK, we were sad to hear she had passed away.

Sand Hills has now reopened and I'm delighted to say Harley is accepting visitors again, as well as donations for his personalised musical performances and tours of the colourful establishment. If you can handle a bit of swearing, and aren't bothered about the possibility of being insulted to your face (all in good spirits of course, but the easily offended, or those travelling with children, may decide to give the shop a miss), make sure you stop by to see this one-of-a-kind Route 66 attraction and its larger-than-life owner.

6
EVERYTHING'S BIGGER IN TEXAS, ESPECIALLY THE STEAK

As you head towards the Texas border, you can drive for miles without another car in sight. The stretch from Erick, Oklahoma, to the state line evokes a real sense of adventure. In the middle of nowhere, Dave and I were free – a young couple tearing along the open road in a red all-American muscle car. What a time to be alive.

This section of the Will Rogers Highway is also a stark reminder of how much Route 66 has changed. Crumbling ghost towns now stand where populations once thrived on the passing tourist trade. Trees burst through the concrete of the original and abandoned 66, which runs parallel to today's road. America's Main Street was realigned many times throughout its history as needs changed and technology advanced. Entire lengths were left to fade into the landscape. The trend continued right until the route was decommissioned in the 1980s, when the Interstate Highway System bypassed its towns and left many to ruin. The holiday-makers stopped coming and the townsfolk moved on to pastures new.

The Texas state line is one of the only border markers on the route where it is 'safe' to stop for a photo. But although you're not on an interstate with fast moving traffic, you'll need to be on the lookout for snakes and spiders as you jump from one state to another. Once you've finished mucking around, head back into the car and onto Shamrock.

I had longed to visit this small Texan town ever since I discovered that its art deco masterpiece, the U Drop Inn, was the inspiration for Ramone's Body Shop in *Cars*. Little did I know then that this building would soon play an important part in my own story.

Also known as the Conoco Tower, Shamrock's U Drop Inn is a former gas station beautifully restored to its 1930s glory. It may be the most stunning gas station in the world. Its exterior is coated in glazed cream and olive green walls, crowned with a geometric zigzag trim, common amongst art deco architecture of the time. There's a tower at either end of the building. One is marked 'Conoco' and advertises the fuel it used to sell, and the other says 'cafe', although the restaurant no longer serves food. On the forecourt, two disused gas pumps still stand and a Route 66 shield is painted onto the floor. At night, orange and green neon lights beam brightly from the roof. It's art deco neon heaven.

So imagine my delight when Dave selected the U Drop Inn, exactly in the centre of the Route 66 shield, under the neon lights, to ask me to marry him.

Now if Dave were to tell you the story of our engagement, it would be ever so slightly different. He'd tell you how worried he'd been going through airport security in case the staff found a diamond ring in his hand luggage, and how the butterflies only intensified as he carried it from motel to motel halfway across America. He'd also tell you he was so nervous that he couldn't eat all of his dinner in Big Vern's Steakhouse, just along from the U Drop Inn (which is a shame as my food was yummy). And that he was thankful that I spent so long in the supermarket up the road choosing a dog toy for Kevin the Tee Pee Curios Pooch (the dog we hoped to visit in New Mexico – more in the next chapter) and spray paint to graffiti cars at the Cadillac Ranch, because it gave him a chance to calm down. He'd tell you the reason he took so many photos of the U Drop Inn lit up in neon lights was because he was practising the lines he'd rehearsed in his head for the last year.

He'd also complain that he had to 'wrestle' me out of the Dodge. I was cold and fed up that he was taking so many photos when I wanted to go back to the hotel. He'd tell you that he tried to get me out the car by asking me to bring him something from the boot, but then gave up after I continued to be a pain in the ass and instead said, 'I need to ask you something.' The whole thing was a lot less romantic than he had planned, but it was ok because I said yes when I finally realised what was happening. And he gets to tell this story, which our friends and family think is hilarious because it sums me up to a tee. And now you're reading about it too. If it had gone any other way, it wouldn't have been 'us'.

The next day we returned to the U Drop Inn to see if we could take a look inside (it was closed the day before). We were delighted to find it just as stunning as its exterior. Make sure you look up at the squared patterned ceiling and take a minute to watch some of *Cars*, which plays on a loop all day. There's a gift shop, replica diner booth, evocative of its cafe days, and the most wonderfully friendly staff. They were delighted to hear all about our engagement on their forecourt – we were the first couple from the UK, and the third overall, to pop the question on their premises. They treated us to a Route 66 Soda each as an engagement present and took some photos for their Facebook page. Teresa, who works there, and I still email each other, and her team sent us a wonderful wedding present (a Route 66 kitchen set) when we finally tied the knot two years later. The U Drop Inn featured on the top tier of our wedding cake, complete with real neon lights.

After bidding the fantastic U Drop Inn staff goodbye for now, we drove onto McLean to visit the Devil's Rope Museum (Kingsley St). Now you could be forgiven for thinking that the world's largest barbed wire museum would be a complete bore (what's so great about jagged metal fencing designed to do some serious bodily harm?) Actually, it's a spectacle not to be missed. You'll find pretty much every type of barbed wire ever created (yes, there is more than one), including those from both World Wars, an assortment of cutters and sculptures made from wire, as well as a collection of Route 66 road signs and other memorabilia.

The museum provides yet more insight into US history, particularly through the lens of land ownership; farmers famously used barbed wire to fence off property they claimed under the Homestead Act – land that nomadic Native Americans could no longer roam free. So although you might not ordinarily give wire fencing a second thought, after a visit to McLean's most famous attraction, you'll see how the stuff had such an oddly profound effect on the history of America, as well as the rest of the world. It's eccentricities like this that make Route 66 such fun in combining the sublime with the absurd – who can resist a photo between two giant balls of barbed wire? Please don't drive by it without a visit. There's even a chance to buy some barbed wire offcuts as a souvenir (just don't put them in your hand luggage)!

Next you'll need to find your way to Amarillo, which is nowhere near as difficult as Tony Christie makes out. On the way you'll pass the Leaning Tower of Groom and an enormous cross (near exit 112 of the I-40), evidencing you're in the Bible Belt.

At the Cadillac Ranch (13651 I-40 Frontage Rd), you'll find a row of cars buried bonnet first in the ground, each apparently at the same angle as the Great Pyramid of Giza (for no known reason). This will all sort of make sense when you're told that the installation is the work of bohemian group The Ant Farm on the instruction of the late (bonkers) billionaire Stanley Marsh, who was known for a number of unusual artworks across Amarillo. Today you can graffiti the cars as part of an ever-evolving piece of art (whatever you spray onto the cars won't be there for long). But make sure you bring your own paint and leave your best shoes in the car – the Cadillacs are in the middle of muddy field. This isn't a manned roadside attraction with gift shop, simply a baffling oddity on the outskirts of Amarillo. If you've been paying attention, you'll already know that you can pick up some spray cans in Shamrock. The Ranch isn't actually on Route 66, so you'll need to take a slight detour along the I-40, take exit 60 and drive along the South Frontage Road to find it.

Another diversion that you won't want to miss is a visit to the Big Texan Steak Ranch (7701 I-40 Access Rd). You can stay the night here too in a motel designed to mimic an old western town. We just went for lunch, but if the outside of the motel is anything to go by, it looks like a lot of fun (rooms have Jacuzzi baths, and there's an outside pool). If you decide to stay elsewhere in town, you can call on the restaurant's famous horned limo service to take you to its door.

The Big Texan is famous as the 'home of the 72-ounce steak' – free if you can eat it in under an hour. It's actually not just the beef that you need to devour in order to score a place in the ranch's Hall of Fame. The rules state you must complete an entire steak dinner, including a baked potato, shrimp cocktail, salad and bread roll. You must eat it all up on a raised platform in front of the entire restaurant next to a countdown clock. But you can take one bite before the challenge starts to check the meat is 'cooked to your satisfaction', and if you don't eat it all, you can take it home.

After looking at a replica 72-ounce dinner in the restaurant's display cabinet, I opted for a six-ounce fillet (that 72-ouncer was bigger than my hand!) An eating challenge is still on my bucket list though, so maybe we'll return one day. Before leaving, we played a few games in the on-site amusements and visited the gift shop to buy an engagement ring substitute because my real one needed to be made smaller when we returned home. When we got outside, we returned to the Dodge to see that its grill had been picked clean of the roadkill bugs we'd collected throughout our journey. We soon saw why – the roadrunner birds in the car park had obviously enjoyed their own BBQ, take-out style, whilst we were chowing down inside.

Downtown Amarillo is full of yet more art deco architecture. Sadly, we missed walking through its 'One Mile Shopping' district. But we did drive through it, and it looked fab, lined with antique and craft shops. Make sure you don't miss it! We also found lots of decorated fibreglass horses scattered throughout the city, and they were fun to take photos with as we followed them along the 'Hoof Prints Trail'. This public artwork of more than 100 horse statues, each created by a local artist, celebrates the American Quarter Horse, a popular breed for the cowboys of the Wild West and the most common type of horse in the USA today.

* * * *

The MidPoint Cafe in Adrian is located exactly halfway between Chicago and LA, marking the 1139th mile of the Route 66 journey. The legendary eatery is famous for its 'Ugly Pies'. Don't worry, the restaurant's slogan is 'Nothing real ugly, just real yummy!'

We arrived at Adrian late afternoon and walked straight out into the middle of the road to take the customary photo on the midpoint marker, painted onto the concrete. It would have been quite dangerous if it wasn't for the fact that Adrian has just 150 residents, and all but one of them were nowhere to be seen. Once we'd taken more selfies than actually necessary, we intended to go inside so Dave could try one of the famous 'Ugly Pies' (no gluten-free options here as far as I'm aware).

To our disappointment, Dennis, the owner at the time (new proprietors Brenda and Carrie took over in 2018), had just closed up and was talking to two people on the front drive. Luckily, he explained that although the cafe was shut, he was going to let the two guests look around its gift shop and asked if we wanted to join them. Having missed the opportunity to try the legendary pies, we couldn't pass-up the chance to take a look at the diner, so quickly followed the group through its doors.

Once inside, the male guest told us his name was John Weiss, Mother Road author and active member of the Route 66 Association in Illinois. He had previously escorted Scottish comedian Billy Connolly along the route during his TV documentary, which prompted Dennis to tell us the tale of Billy's legacy to the MidPoint. When he took over the restaurant in 2012, Dennis was told he could no longer call the cafe's popular dessert by its original title. He was forced to choose a new name for the dish and sensibly settled on the 'MidPoint Pie'. When Billy released his book to accompany the TV series, he mistakenly used the term 'ugly pie' to describe the pudding – a sort of hybrid between the original and new name. The slip-up inadvertently renamed the dish, and soon visitors were asking for the famous 'MidPoint Ugly Pie'. The name has stuck to this day.

When Dennis decided that he really did need to close the shop, John asked us if we had time to see another of Adrian's eccentricities. Not ones to turn down offers from esteemed Route 66 historians, we jumped in the car and followed him a few minutes up the road to The Bent Door Cafe. A former restaurant now long fallen into disrepair (although you can donate to the GoFundMe campaign to help restore it), the Bent Door is named so because, you guessed it, it has a wonky door. Why? John explained that the cafe is made from a repurposed aircraft control tower. This becomes clear as soon as you see the slanted windows, which would have been used to monitor planes.

If that wasn't odd enough, just along from the building is a yellow road sign marked 'CROCK OF GIN'. It is part of a series of mad signage put up across Amarillo and the surrounding areas, collectively known as the Dynamite Museum. The project was commissioned by Stanley Marsh of Cadillac Ranch fame. This was the only one we saw of the rumoured 5,000 similar signs, which bear slogans such as 'Twinkle, twinkle little lamb, someone dipped you in mint jam' and 'The world is my apple'. It may well be the only one we ever see – there are calls for any art connected to Marsh to be removed after he was criminally indicted on claims of child sexual assault.

Before leaving the Lone Star State, take the short ride to Glenrio for the sharpest example of the devastating effect of the interstate bypass on Route 66. Now just a row of decaying and vacant shops, gas stations and homes, the once thriving stopover has a population of zero. The ghost town lies across the Texas and New Mexico border and is both sad and eerie. Take a drive through and sit to reflect for a while, but don't venture outside your vehicle. This is desert country and that means snakes and spiders!

7
MARGARITAS, MOVIE STAR MOTELS AND A POOCH NAMED KEVIN IN NEW MEXICO

Behind a pale blue door, a vintage dial telephone sits upon a wooden table, proudly placed on a 1940s hardwood floor. On one side of the parlour, an antique Zenith radio stands tall. On the other, a light brown divan looks on at the TV.

Through the doorway and into the bedroom, a curved mirror forms the centre of an elegant 1937 dressing table. It matches the vintage queen-sized bed, laid with floral duvet and pillows and bearing two white dressing gowns embellished with a small blue and pink logo. Across the room, and separate from the mosaic floored bathroom, is a pale pink clawfoot tub with lavender bath salts and two glasses waiting to be filled with cool white wine. This is room eight, the Lillian Redman Suite, and 'the finest accommodation available at the Blue Swallow Motel' – the star of Route 66 in Tucumcari New Mexico.

Home to just 12 rooms, each painted with a dusty pink

exterior and featuring a personal garage complete with sky blue door, the Blue Swallow Motel has been a beacon of hospitality since 1939. Each room has unique decor, but all sit upon a welcoming forecourt which proudly houses one of the most beautiful neon signs of all the Mother Road. The sign is illuminated every evening, but as one of the most popular stops on Route 66, the word 'vacancies' is rarely lit up. We booked directly with the motel well over six months before arriving. Reserve ahead so you don't miss out.

The motel has had several owners in its lifetime. The most famous is certainly Lillian Redman, after whom the establishment's flagship suite, and our home for our one-night stay, takes its name. Lillian, who sadly passed away in 1999, owned the Blue Swallow for almost 40 years after her soon-to-be husband, Floyd Redman, bought it for her as an engagement present. She is still regarded as one of the route's most welcoming hosts; she used to bless each of her guest rooms with a note, given to every person who checked in. Today the 'benediction' is placed in every room, marking her legacy:

Greetings Traveler:

In ancient times, there was a prayer for "The Stranger Within our Gates." Because this motel is a human institution to serve people, and not solely a money-making organization, we hope that God will grant you peace and rest while you are under our roof.

May this room and motel be your "second" home. May those you love be near you in thoughts and dreams. Even though we may not get to know you, we hope that you will be as comfortable and happy as if you were in your own house.

May the business that brought you this way prosper. May every call you make and every message you receive add to your joy. When you leave, may your journey be safe.

We are all travelers. From "birth till death," we travel between the eternities. May these days be pleasant for you, profitable for society, helpful for those you meet, and a joy to those you know and love best.

Sincerely yours, Lillian Redman

It's one of the loveliest, most genuine, things I've ever read. It touched Dave and me so much that we included it as a note in each of our guests' rooms at our Route-66-inspired wedding.

Fortunately, hosts Nancy and Kevin were every bit as welcoming during our visit (I hope the new owners will be too, as the motel was up for sale again at the time of writing). Nancy, and her gorgeous golden retriever, Bessie, greeted us with a warm smile before showing us around our room. She suggested that we reserve a space on the free shuttle bus to take us to a nearby (New) Mexican restaurant later that evening and happily booked us a ride after we gladly accepted the chance to indulge in the local cuisine.

When dinner time arrived, we were joined by two ladies from Sunderland, UK. We had so much fun laughing with them on the short taxi ride that we decided to share a table when we arrived at the Pow Wow Restaurant and Lizard Lounge (801 W Route 66). Being in New Mexico it was only right that I joined everyone in trying my first margarita, an action that's been responsible for my love affair with the cocktail ever since. By all accounts, the food was delicious too and rather spicy. The tacos soaked up my margarita nicely, but you'll also find a great selection of fajitas, enchiladas, fish and grills to choose from.

The walls of the restaurant are covered with hand-painted pictures. So far on our trip, we'd seen lots of murals in Route 66 towns so, apart from being particularly fun and colourful examples, we didn't think too much about these until the waitress came over to explain more. She drew our attention to a painting of an elderly couple sitting at a table and asked us if we noticed anything unusual. After trying hard to spot an abnormality, we gave up. Smiling, the waitress pointed to a table across the restaurant. There, sat opposite each other and tucking into an evening meal, was the living embodiment of the mural – the real-life couple featured in the painting. The pair had been coming to the Pow Wow to eat for years, so the owners decided to paint a tribute to them on the wall. To our delight, they moved to the booth to recreate the exact scene so we could take a photo!

The following morning, it was time to check out of the Lillian Redman Suite, so we headed into the reception (and gift shop) to say goodbye to Nancy and return our key. Nancy asked us how our stay was and, remarking on the fact that we were British, she enquired into how we were coping travelling so far without regular cups of tea. Now, Americans are predominantly coffee drinkers, so the closest thing we'd had to a brew in the last 1,500 or so miles was the sweet iced variety, and I had to admit that I was dying for a proper cuppa. Laughing, Nancy took us over to the hostess trolley she kept especially for Brits like us. It was packed with different brands of English breakfast tea, and we were welcome to a cup of whatever we desired.

At the sight of the table, I can only imagine that I looked like a lost desert traveller who had suddenly found a lake, because, seeing my beaming smile, Nancy exclaimed that she had a treat for real tea fans – a cup of 'the Queen's tea'. She ran off into her pantry to fetch some (a gift, she explained, from another British traveller). Unfortunately, when she returned, Dave and I burst out laughing; the 'Queen's tea' turned out to be Asda Smart Price. Luckily, she saw the funny side when we explained she was holding the equivalent of Walmart produce and informed her that the Queen actually drinks Twinings. We stopped and had a cuppa with her and Bessie before heading off to visit her friends across the road.

Now remember back in Texas (before Dave proposed)

that we stopped by the supermarket to buy a dog toy? Kevin, the Tee Pee Curios Pooch, was the reason why. Believed to be a mix of Corgi and German shepherd, according to his Facebook page, Kevin is 'security guard and head people greeter' at Tucumcari's curiosity shop, Tee Pee Curios (named so because you walk through a teepee to enter it). The shop owners claim Kevin adopted them when he turned up there in 2013, and he's stayed ever since.

Except, it seems, on the day that Dave and I had scheduled to visit; after following the four-legged friend on Facebook for months before our trip, I was devastated that Kevin had decided to stay home when we stopped by. His mummy, Heidi Engman, was ill and Kevin was looking after her, so I couldn't be sad for long. I gave his toy to owner Gar Engman, and he gave us a postcard as a thank you. Later that day I saw just how happy Kevin was with his new toy after he decided to share it with the world in a Facebook post. Make sure you stop by and visit the whole family to stock up on souvenirs, from rattlesnake mugs and slogan T-shirts to handmade teepee ornaments and Route 66 oven mittens.

After leaving Tucumcari, you have a decision to make just after Santa Rosa. Head straight on through Albuquerque on post-1937 Route 66, driving mostly I-40 (an option if you don't have much time), or take the Santa Fe Loop on the pre-1937 stretch. Dave and I opted for the latter, longer of the two and, if time allows, would suggest you do the same to make sure you don't miss a very different side of Route 66. This is a decision best planned in advance, though, as it did add two days to our trip.

Although America's Main Street changed route many times before its decommission in 1985, rumour has it that the reason for bypassing the New Mexico state capital was not purely due to efficiency. It was at this time that A. T. Hannett failed to be re-elected as governor. Angry with Santa Fe politicians, who he blamed for losing him the election, Hannett took revenge by re-routing the popular highway through Albuquerque, bypassing Santa Fe businesses and, I imagine, costing the city quite a deal in lost tourist trade. But what you rack up in the additional 90 or so miles you gain in beautiful scenery; the Santa Fe Loop is lined with mountain views and vast open plains.

But be ready for a culture shock when you arrive into the city. Unlike the neon lights and 1930s architecture of much of Route 66, the United States' oldest state capital, Santa Fe, is filled with an abundance of well-preserved reddish brown buildings made of mud and straw. These buildings were created by Spanish settlers improving on the designs of the original Native American inhabitants. As such, Santa Fe is home to the oldest house, building and church in the USA, all of which you can visit.

As well as this rich display of Pueblo-style architecture, Santa Fe is famous for inspiring many paintings by American artist Georgia O'Keeffe. You can see the world's largest permanent collection of her work, including the famous *Ram's Head, Blue Morning Glory*, in The Georgia O'Keeffe Museum (217 Johnson St) in the city. Afterwards, head to the Loretto Chapel (207 Old Santa Fe Trail) to see the Miraculous Staircase, carved from a single piece of wood by a mystery man. Its carpenter is believed to have arrived unannounced at the church looking for employment and seemingly answered the prayers of the chapel's nuns, who were struggling to find a way to reach its loft. But that's not the only oddity surrounding the staircase – it was made without nails or any central support. The chapel has featured in numerous TV programmes, films and articles, with the creator of its famous staircase still unverified.

After leaving the city, you might decide to take a ride up the Sandia Peak Aerial Tramway (30 Tramway Road, Albuquerque). Despite being pre-warned that Santa Fe's thin air takes time to adjust to (the city is 7,199 feet above sea level), I wasn't prepared for the resulting altitude sickness I experienced halfway up America's longest aerial tram.

By the time we'd reached the top of the 10,000-foot trip to Sandia Peak, I was struggling not to faint, especially when the peak was 20 degrees cooler at its top than at the bottom (pack a jumper). Thankfully, I managed to exit the tram in just enough time to take a seat and catch my breath. I was quite proud of myself for coping without needing to use an oxygen tank; apparently I was the third person that morning to experience 'acute mountain sickness' (AMS), as the affliction is commonly known, but the only one to sort myself out without additional aids. My advice is to stay hydrated (even more than usual – bring a bottle on board), and if you have low blood pressure, or struggle with heights, give the tram a miss.

By the time I'd recovered from my dizziness, all I managed was a very short walk around the top of the mountain before I couldn't bear the limited oxygen and took the tram back down again. On the bright side, we didn't encounter any forest fires, bears, bobcats or mountain lions, as the sign at the tram entrance warned, and I met a lovely lady in the restroom who had lived in Wethersfield, Essex (a village near my hometown) for four years. Thus I didn't have a completely wasted trip.

For those who don't suffer from AMS, Dave assures me that the view from the top is worth the $25 (approximately £18 in 2018) return trip. Spikey peaks of granite sit amongst luscious greenery, and it's possible to see up to 11,000 square miles across the Rio Grande Valley on a good day. There's a number of viewing platforms to look out from and, if you've brought suitable footwear, you could visit one of the hiking trails. On your way back down, you can make out the remains of TWA Flight 260, if you look closely enough, which killed 16 people when the plane crashed into the mountain during the 1950s.

Once Dave had recovered from nearly losing his fiancé

to oxygen starvation, he drove us into downtown Albuquerque. Although the city's stretch of Route 66 is undoubtably beautiful, especially the Kimo Theatre (423 Central) in the Pueblo deco style, this was the first town on our adventure where we didn't feel safe.

Now if you do a bit of googling, you'll see that the jury is out on whether or not Albuquerque is any less safe than any other US city. Please do your research and make up your own mind as to whether you feel comfortable or not visiting, or whether you decide just to stay in your vehicle. I can only tell you our experiences and opinions of this part of Route 66 – but remember we were only there for a few hours.

We walked past six or seven groups of men celebrating because they had just been released from prison and, at lunch time, we were served meatloaf by a gentleman with beaten-up knuckles. We should, of course, know better than to stereotype, but we decided to trust our gut instinct. After a quick oil change at a local garage (it's likely you'll need one too if you're driving a muscle car the length of 66), we decided on a swift exit. It's likely we were overreacting (and we left the place unharmed), but Albuquerque is not a city we'd return to in a hurry.

However, the drive to Gallup, the next town on our agenda, was exceptional (although we encountered some less than patient drivers). The landscape got increasingly stunning as we drove, the road framed by huge red stone mountains and mile-long freight trains.

We arrived at 'America's Most Patriotic Town' late in the evening, so it was early to bed following a quick meal at Denny's. The next morning, we were delighted to have the opportunity to eat breakfast at the El Rancho Hotel (1000 E Hwy 66), 'Home of the movie stars'.

Although we'd thought we'd done a pretty good job planning our 66 trip, somehow we missed booking this Mother Road landmark, so a meal in its restaurant would have to suffice (please don't make the same mistake and book early to avoid the disappointment we experienced). But after a delicious plate of steak and eggs (much to Dave's amusement at my ability to pack away a main meal that early in the day), we did get the chance to look at the hotel lobby.

The El Rancho is famous as the luxury hotel of Route 66's heyday, frequented by Hollywood's elite. Doris Day, James Cagney and Humphrey Bogart are amongst the long list of yesteryear celebs who checked into the hotel when filming westerns nearby. The interior, from what we saw, was exquisite, with a dark wooden staircase and stag heads protruding from the walls.

Downtown, the community's American pride is evidenced by a large 'Gallup' sign painted in Stars and Stripes. On the front of the town's chamber of commerce building, you can also see a neon mural of a pink Cadillac driving along Route 66, created by the author of the *EZ Guide*, Jerry McClanahan. The area also features a host of art galleries and trading posts, selling an abundance of Navajo rugs, pottery and jewellery at reasonable prices, so a trip into town is well worth stretching your legs for before you head to Arizona.

8
DONKEYS, DINOSAURS AND DETOURS IN ARIZONA AND LAS VEGAS

When I first heard about the Petrified Forest, I pictured something akin to the dark and thorny moors from *Maleficent*. The name certainly sounds like a Disney creation and, after all we'd seen so far on Route 66, an enchanted forest in the middle of the desert didn't seem that farfetched. But this wood really is magical; all of its trees have turned into stone.

Approximately 25 miles outside of Holbrook, the Arizona Petrified Forest National Park and the Painted Desert are two of the finest examples of nature's wizardry. The vast open space is littered with fossilised fallen trees, turned into colourful rock through millions of years of sedimentation. The process began after volcanic eruptions swept the trees away, covering them with ash and, later, water. Gradual erosion eventually exposed the 'logs', revealing gorgeous pink and red quartz. The petrified wood sits on top of a rainbow of brightly coloured earth, in layered mounds of purple, red, orange and pink. It looks like Mother Nature has taken a paintbrush to the hills.

As well as being a marvel of the natural world, the Painted Desert was once home to an alignment of Route 66. Today, all that's left of the abandoned stretch is a row of forgotten telegraph poles. Grass and tumbleweed have grown over the road completely, making for an eerie photo opportunity. But make sure that's your only souvenir from this attraction – the petrified wood is fiercely protected, so don't pick any up from the desert floor. If you really want some of this fossilised nature, you'll find plenty legitimately sourced and reasonably priced in the gift shop or trading posts on the outskirts of the park.

The Painted Desert Inn is another of the park's Route 66 relics (originally made from petrified wood, but now restored with 1930s adobe mud). The inn has been repurposed as a museum, so you can't sleep or eat here anymore, but it's worth a visit to see an example of Pueblo revival architecture and look around the exhibits inside. The museum features a number of Navajo quilts and murals on its walls and is set out to give you a flavour of what it might have been like to stay at the inn all those years ago. There's not a huge amount of information on offer inside, but you will get a spectacular view of the desert from the veranda. Elsewhere in the park, be sure not to miss Agate Bridge – a huge fallen petrified tree that has formed a natural walkway across a desert rim.

After leaving the Petrified Forest, why not indulge in a spot of dinosaur hunting? Don't worry, though. Although these dinosaurs are certainly large, they are definitely inanimate. Holbrook and its surrounding areas capitalise on their prehistoric history by lining the forecourts of pretty much any shop with huge monster statutes in the hope of enticing roadies to buy their wares (mostly more petrified wood). Jim Gray's Petrified Wood Co (147 US-180) has some fantastic dinosaur statues, including an enormous T-rex and what I think are meant to be a selection of velociraptors (who appear to be smiling, weirdly), but the best, in my opinion, are at the Rainbow Rock Shop (Navajo Blvd) just as you enter Holbrook. Here you can see a giant diplodocus!

More dinosaurs await at Stewarts Rock Shop (9406 Washboard Rd), but unfortunately this was one trading post we missed. We had a pretty good go at trying to find it, but it turned out we'd driven around 50 miles in the wrong direction. However, we did find the Geronimo Trading Post (5372 Geronimo Road) upon our return to Holbrook, meaning we got to see the world's largest petrified tree.

Holbrook isn't only famous for its dinosaurs. This small town also provides the chance to sleep in a concrete teepee. Built in 1950, the Wigwam Motel (811 W Hopi Dr.) was originally part of a chain of seven motor courts constructed of individual teepee sleeping units. Only two remain in the US, making a stay in the Holbrook establishment a must for any Route 66 traveller (book direct and in advance). Each teepee contains a basic, but larger than expected, bedroom, bathroom and an old American car standing on its drive. In the evening, we drank cold beers on a bench outside the wigwam's door.

The motel's strapline asks 'Have you slept in a wigwam lately?' Unfortunately, I have to answer no; train tracks lay directly behind our room and we were woken by passing freights throughout the night. However, a stay here is a novelty and an experience we would do again in a heartbeat. *Cars* fans will also recognise similarities with Sally's Cosy Cone Motel, and surely that's worth a little bit of broken sleep?

Cars owes a lot to Holbrook, as we discovered later that evening at nearby Mexican, Joe and Aggie's Cafe (120 W Hopi Dr.). After sampling some insanely hot 'chile' (the restaurant's signature dish in a choice of either green or red), we went over to look at some memorabilia crammed into the corner of the main reception. By now I'm sure you can imagine our delight when we spotted a film poster signed by Pixar's John Lasseter, as well as a film release form – former owner Stanley was immortalised in the film as the founder of Radiator Springs, the fictional town Lightning McQueen finds himself in after getting lost along Route 66. We spent hours talking to Stanley's son about the film and how Pixar visited the restaurant during research for the movie. It was one of our favourite evenings of the trip; the Route 66 shield pin badges we bought there featured in our wedding flowers.

* * * *

As you approach the Jack Rabbit Trading Post (3386 Route 66) just outside Joseph City, a huge yellow billboard proclaims 'HERE IT IS!' In the Mother Road's heyday, similar signs could be found for hundreds of miles along the highway, each counting down the distance until road warriors would arrive at the curiosity shop. Its unique style of advertising has made the store somewhat of a Route 66 legend; *Cars* fans, look out for a parody in the film, this time featuring a Ford Model T on the yellow sign.

The shop was shut when we arrived early in the morning. Rather than be disappointed, we decided to use the opportunity to take some photos, especially aboard the fibreglass jackrabbit statue on the forecourt. We met an American couple doing the route from west to east on two Harleys and offered to take their photo. By the time we'd finished snapping, the shop's owner had arrived to open up! We left with postcards, pin badges and a jar of cactus jam, and headed back on the road to Winslow.

Even if you're not a fan of the Eagles, taking a photo on the corner of Winslow, Arizona, is still a lot of fun. Based on just one verse of their song 'Take it Easy', the town has paid tribute to those few short lyrics with a mural, a statue of a man standing on the corner and, of course, a girl in a flat-bed Ford. Winslow also added a monument to singer Glenn Frey, after he passed away in 2016. Across the road, a giant Route 66 shield is painted onto the concrete. The town also boasts a number of places to eat, as well as classic motels (including the large, and beautiful, Spanish-inspired La Posada on East 2nd Street) and decaying retro gas stations and diners.

Next, it was onto another famous landmark, although this time of nature rather than popular culture. Just off exit 233 of I-40, you'll find a genuine meteor crater. This giant hole in the ground is the Earth's best-preserved meteorite impact site, nearly one mile across. You can check it out at one of a number of viewing points on the site, and the attraction also features an informative museum and gift shop.

A few miles on from the crater, we made a quick stop by the Two Arrows (exit 219). These huge wooden structures once belonged to a popular diner, which has long shut, resulting in the arrows being barricaded behind a concrete wall. You can still get a good photo, but do not trespass over the wall; the private land belongs to the Hopi tribe.

* * * *

Flagstaff is perhaps best known as a stopover for tourists visiting the nearby Grand Canyon. However, it's also home to some fantastic examples of Route 66 eccentricity, with The Museum Club (3404 E Route 66) being just one of them. This restaurant and bar was originally a taxidermy museum but, although stuffed animals can be found hanging from its walls, the watering hole is now predominately used as a live music venue. It's rumoured to be both haunted and the largest log cabin in Arizona. We arrived in the afternoon, so we didn't spot any ghosts, or bands for that matter, but it was still great for a drink. If you're staying in Flagstaff (unlike us), I imagine The Museum Club would be even more fun to visit in the evening. The staff are friendly and the beer is good – what more can you ask for?

Downtown, we stopped for a photo with Tall Paul, a smaller replica of a Muffler Man that used to stand on the forecourt of the Lumberjack Cafe. The restaurant was succeeded by Granny's Closet (218 S Milton Rd), but at the time of writing, the eatery has been put up for auction. Elsewhere in Flagstaff, you'll find colourful buildings and a lively, almost festival-like, atmosphere (from what we gathered, this is where hikers let off steam after a hard day walking through the Canyon). It was the busiest town we'd visited so far and was full of young people, many of whom were riding cycle-powered mobile bars around the streets! If that's anything to go by, I can see the nightlife being quite enjoyable, but we had accommodation booked inside the Grand Canyon National Park, so we didn't get to experience it. This is something to consider when deciding where to sleep if you opt for a detour to this marvel of nature.

The Grand Canyon isn't actually on Route 66. But when you've driven more than 1,500 miles to a town just outside one of the Seven Wonders of the Natural World, it seems silly not to pay it a visit, provided you've factored in the time. You can access the National Park via either the North or South Rim, or visit the Hualapai tribe-owned Grand Canyon West and dare yourself to look down from the glass-bottomed Skywalk (for an additional fee). Your choice depends on how much time you have (the North Rim involves around a four-hour drive from Flagstaff), the time of year you travel (the North Rim is only open May to October) and what you want to achieve from your visit (the South Rim is the more 'touristy' side, with a greater choice of hotels and restaurants). It's also important to note that if you decide to visit Grand Canyon West, you'll need to do so further into your itinerary (taking the turn just after Hackberry) so you don't miss some fantastic Route 66 towns on the way. We opted for the South Rim, around an hour and a half's drive from Flagstaff, to make best use of time.

After stocking up on fluids (bottled water is no longer sold inside the park, but there are refill stations), we headed to the National Geographic Visitor Center (450 AZ-64, Grand Canyon Village) to buy our entrance passes (you can also purchase tours here) – we hear buying them at the entrance gate means waiting in a long queue. It costs $30 per car to enter the park, which must be paid in addition to any accommodation you book inside.

We didn't actually find any queues when we arrived in the early evening. This was just as well given our traumatic drive from Flagstaff, when the heavens opened with a huge hail storm that covered the road in ice. In a matter of minutes, it looked like it had been snowing for days. Given that our muscle car tyres weren't designed for blizzard conditions, we spent quite a lot of time sliding along the highway until we eventually pulled off into a service station. The hail was soon over as quick as it started, the ice melted and we were on our way again, but it certainly felt hairy at the time. So be prepared!

The South Rim has a range of accommodation to choose from if you've decided to stay inside the park, from camping and RV parking to a number of hotels. If you're planning to hike below the canyon's rim, there are also campsites on the designated trails, but you need a Backcountry Permit to stay in them. These are difficult to obtain, and you must apply for them four months in advance via fax or post to the Backcountry Information Center. Staying inside the park is hugely popular, so I can't stress enough the importance of doing your research and booking at least six months in advance.

You'll need to book even earlier if you want to stay in the El Tovar. First opened in 1905, the lodging is the park's original hotel and sits right on the rim of the canyon. It was originally owned and run by the Fred Harvey Company, which operated a number of establishments along the Santa Fe railway. The El Tovar is designated a National Historic Landmark and is constructed of beautiful, dark Oregon pine in the style of a log cabin. It was the height of luxury for early 20th-century travellers, with an elegant dining room, gorgeous lighting and mounted animal heads on the walls. The hotel is just as stunning today, but with only 78 rooms, a stay here can be difficult to obtain.

I'm still not sure if the story of how Dave and I bagged the El Tovar's Bellboy Suite is something to be proud or embarrassed about. I'll caveat by saying that, other than the Blue Swallow Motel, it was the place we wanted to stay the most on our trip. So, when we tried to make a reservation nine months beforehand, you can imagine our disappointment when we were told the hotel was fully booked. Having a sister-in-law who worked in the hospitality sector, Dave knew that hotels often keep certain rooms aside in case the world's rich and famous need to make a last-minute reservation, so he called the El Tovar to see if this was the case for them too.

A long, international phone call later, and the El Tovar had booked famous British racing car driver, David Graves, into one of its special suites. Of course Dave neglected to mention that although he had been on TV, it was just the once, and that his championship is a club sport hobby rather than a profession, but the mind can be particularly imaginative when needs must. So if you can't book the hotel first time round, you might decide to resort to creative negotiation (although now I've ruined the trade secret, I can't guarantee it will work!).

After a bellboy carried our bags to our room (!), we headed to the hotel bar for a pre-dinner drink to watch the sunset overlooking the canyon's edge. It was raining heavily, which affected our view. Our disappointment didn't last long, though, as we were soon treated to spectacular sights of sheet lightning across the canyon as we sipped our cocktails. Dinner was buffalo steak in the exquisite El Tovar Dining Room, which we reserved six months in advance to avoid disappointment. It was pricey but fabulous (like the hotel) and not to be missed if you do decide to stay here.

The next morning we were up extremely early to see the sunrise over the canyon at Yakapi Point – do your homework and find out the sunrise and set times on the park's website before you arrive. Next it was on to breakfast at the Bright Angel Restaurant, also in the historic district, for huevos rancheros (Mexican breakfast of tacos, refried beans, eggs and olives) – the Americans know how to eat!

If you want to hike inside the canyon, it's important to plan in advance. You'll need to check the weather (lightning storms have been known to kill here), make sure you have enough water, wear the correct clothes to protect yourself from the heat and plan your route. The best day hike is the Bright Angel Trail (seven miles from the rim to the Colorado River), but it's advised not to trek the entire way there and back in a day – it takes twice as long to ascend as it does descend. Hiking in the canyon really isn't something to be taken lightly (people have lost their lives by getting lost or exhausted), so do your research and take it easy. There are also all sorts of organised trips, including jeep and horse rides that you can book online in advance, as well as free Ranger programmes where you can turn up on the day. Check out the park's website for more information (but be patient – it's a bit difficult to navigate).

With just one full day in the canyon, we decided to stick to the rim and took the free shuttle bus to the end of Hermit's Rest Trail (this road is closed to private traffic so is less congested). It's an eight-mile walk back from here to the Grand Canyon Village (the centre of tourist activity), but we alternated walking along the edge with short stints on the hop-on, hop-off shuttle. Along our way we spotted mule deer, elks, a condor and a ground squirrel making the most insane noise that resonated across the canyon (the park recommends you stay at least 100 feet away from large animals and 50 feet away from smaller ones - it is illegal to feed or harass any of them). Down below, the Colorado River rapids looked like they weren't even moving because we were so far above them.

If you fancy a day off from driving, you can also get to the South Rim by train using the Grand Canyon Railway (there's even a Wild West show beforehand!) It departs daily from 9.30 a.m. at Williams, the last original Route 66 town to be bypassed by I-40. From 13 October 1984, travellers can journey the entire way from Chicago to LA by interstate, without needing to visit America's small towns.

Williams is a must-stop destination for any Route 66 traveller. We arrived in the afternoon, checked into the Ramanda (free popcorn in the lobby!) and set off downtown to the 'wrong side of the tracks'. You'll soon see why when you spot the Red Garter Inn, a former brothel turned haunted bed and breakfast. The hotel's website says that tales of Eve, the ghost of a young girl, whose identity is unknown, are overblown, but guest have reported their beds being shaken and even a hand touching them at night. The hotel had a particularly colourful past, once housing an opium den run by Chinese railroad workers and even being the site of a murder in the 1940s.

Saloon Row, the area of Railroad Avenue which houses the Red Garter, along with other bars, gambling houses and opium dens back in the day, soon earned Williams a reputation as a rowdy cowboy town. But Williams is now better known as one of the best examples of retro Americana of all Route 66. Its compact downtown is packed with gift shops, diners and motels, with not an abandoned building in sight. Stop by Pete's Gas Station Museum to see a gorgeous example of art deco architecture, filled to the brim with Route 66 merchandise, and spend some time exploring the trading posts along Main Street. There are tonnes of places to eat, but expect to pay a little more here than other 66 towns – the roaring tourist trade means Williams can hike up the prices. You'd also be smart to book any accommodation well ahead, especially in high season.

Because you'll certainly want to stay overnight in Williams. An evening walk here is pure joy for vintage fans. Neon signs gleam back at you from both sides of the road. Even better is a slow cruise round the downtown ring, driving slowly eastbound along Route 66 on a one-way road (with 'Sh-Boom' by The Chords blearing from the stereo if you're like Dave and me), before looping back down Railroad Avenue to do it all over again, just to take it all in. Aside from Flagstaff, Williams is the liveliest town along the route (only two restaurants were closed on the night we visited, and they were only shut because it was a Sunday). It's abundance of bright lights and burgeoning businesses is the closest thing you'll get to feeling what a thriving Route 66 might have been like in its heyday. So soak up the atmosphere.

The treats continue as you approach Seligman, famous for kick-starting the movement to preserve and protect Historic Route 66. As you near the town, you'll be greeted by a series of satirical four-line poems. These signs are replicas of the famous Burma-Shave billboards which lined America's roadsides from the 1920s until the 1950s (although, ironically, they were not originally found in Arizona). Burma-Shave used the somewhat sarcastic rhymes as a successful advertising tactic for its brushless shaving cream. Today they are just a lot of fun to look and laugh at.

We arrived at Seligman early to see the town before the herds of tourists arrived (and boy did they arrive later). We headed straight to Angel and Velma's barbershop, now the Route 66 Visitor Center, complete with an original barber's chair and letters from fans around the world. It was here we came face-to-face with the legend himself; I hope you too get to meet the Angel of Route 66 and appreciate just how much he's done for you. It's thanks to Angel that you can take this trip of a lifetime.

Right next door to the barbershop, you'll find the Hulk's head emerging from a toilet. This is the forecourt of the Snow Cap, which serves tacos, burritos and 'dead chicken' according to the sign outside. The restaurant was the brainchild of Angel's brother, Juan Delgadillo, who delighted in enticing in customers with his odd assortment of props before playing tricks on them when they ordered food. Juan passed away many years ago, but the restaurant is now run by his daughter. We had to leave before it opened during our visit (one of the downsides of getting to Seligman early). I hear it's not to be missed, so stick around and sample that dead chicken.

It only gets madder as you head through town. A plane has crashed into the roof of Seligman Sundries and mannequins in cocktail dresses pose seductively on top of the Rusty Bolt and Thunderbird Indian Store, whilst a man in a hat points a gun at them from the window. The plastic dolls are redressed and re-posed every so often to add to the spectacle. At Copper Cart, you can sign a VW campervan resembling Fillmore, the hippie Transporter bus from *Cars* – Radiator Springs very clearly evokes the Seligman vibe.

Cars' creators also appear to have taken inspiration from the Hackberry General Store, further along the route. The red 1956 Corvette outside features the same paint job and whitewall tyres that Lightning McQueen emerges with from Ramone's Body Shop after he's fixed the road. This store was formerly owned by Bob Waldmire, of Pontiac, Illinois fame, and features authentic Burma-Shave signs, a number of old cars and road signs on its forecourt. Men can enjoy some 'unique' wallpaper in the restroom too. There's plenty to see in the shop and lots of great photo opportunities, so make sure you stop by before heading to Kingman to fill up on petrol (it's a long way until the next gas station).

The Oatman Highway has a reputation for being a notoriously dangerous part of Route 66; the large number of deadly accidents on its Sitgreaves Pass was one of the reasons behind the 'Bloody 66' nickname up until the 1950s. But if the weather is good and you're a confident driver, you'll be absolutely fine. As the US is famed for its long straight roads (it's one of the reasons driving Route 66 is so much fun), I imagine that a curving, ascending stretch of concrete (with some sizable drops) could be quite a shock for Americans driving the route. But anyone who has driven through the Peak District or the Welsh mountain roads can tackle the Oatman Highway. Just drive slowly. Cars only, though – RVs will need to take the I-40.

A trip along the Oatman Highway really is worth it. You'll be treated to fantastic views, gorgeous desert landscape and an experience like no other on Route 66. But by far the best part awaits you when you eventually reach Oatman itself, which seems to spring up out of the landscape from nowhere. Just like that, we were back in the Wild West. Originally a mining town, Oatman relives its cowboy days with staged gun fights, saloons and western-themed gift shops and bars. The town looks like a set from a Wild West theme park. In September, try to be there for lunchtime as you can only rely on the noon gun show on quiet days.

But Oatman's main tourist attraction is definitely its 'wild burros' (donkeys to you and me). When the Gold Rush ended and the miners no longer needed their mules, they set them free. But although the miners left, the burros stayed, and now Oatman is treated to a daily visit from its furry friends who take over every inch of the town by day and escape to the mountains at night. And the donkeys are everywhere – in the road, on the paths, inside its shops – and in our car, after Dave opened my window and one stuck it's head right inside. When we were able to get out of the Dodge to open the boot, sure enough a burro stuck its head right in there too. We were lucky enough to meet a foal who was just five days old as he struggled to move away from a shopkeeper who was going in for a stroke. But foals learn quickly, and, as soon as this baby realised that strokes felt good, he was following him around the shop for more! Feel free to touch, but do be careful: wild burros can bite!

* * * *

Nevada is not one of the eight Route 66 states, but it's around a two-hour drive from Needles (the first Mother Road town in California) so it made sense to add a visit to Las Vegas to our itinerary. Unfortunately, the trip involves a boring drive down the very straight US-95, which is less than thrilling after the bends of the Oatman Highway. At least the tiny tornados of Nevada desert sand gave us something to look at.

After the small towns of Route 66 and their good old-fashioned mom-and-pop hospitality, Las Vegas was a huge shock to the system. I think we were expecting some sort of Disney World for adults, but what we actually experienced felt closer to Banksy's Dismaland.

From the stretch limousines to the world's biggest slot machine and huge frozen cocktails, everything was about being big and bolshie – a place for showing off the size of your wallet rather than the size of your heart. In Vegas, I felt like I was only worth what I could afford to pay (in one restaurant, it seemed like the waiters sat us at the back because we were young and underdressed, and therefore, in their eyes, unlikely to tip). Homeless people were ignored as they begged on the bridges over the strip, and men walked the streets handling out cards with telephone numbers to call 'girls to your room'.

Now our judgement is likely to have been clouded by weeks spent in a nostalgic Americana bubble. Maybe if we went to Las Vegas again on a 'city break', we'd see things differently (although friends who have recently visited said they felt the same as us). But despite all this, we did have a good time. We felt extremely safe, and there's nothing dirty or seedy about the strip (if you're looking for that, maybe call the number on one of those cards?) Seeing as you might also like to experience Vegas for yourself, our few days spent there are worth recounting.

To continue our theme of sleeping in pyramid-shaped establishments, we chose to stay in the Luxor. Vegas hotels have resort fees, extra compulsory charges for the use of hotel facilities, and these vary between $11 and $39 (£8 and £28 in 2018) plus tax a night, so do your research before you book to avoid unexpected costs. After checking into our room, facing the strip and offering fantastic views of the sunset, we headed out to watch a volcano erupt at the Mirage and then the Bellagio fountains (every 15 minutes in the evening). To get a feel of the place, we set off on a walk to the Stratosphere, a hotel at the very end of the strip with a theme park on its roof, and made the classic rookie error – it's an eight-mile walk along the strip there and back! We didn't discover the bus until the next day, so please don't make the same mistake, unless you enjoy long walks in intense heat.

We spent three days in Vegas and found lots to do, including a pre-booked passenger ride in a NASCAR at Las Vegas Motor Speedway to celebrate Dave's 30th (visit the Richard Petty website for options). We had a laugh aboard a gondola inside the Venetian, where we were serenaded by a man pretending to row what was actually a motorised boat travelling along a shopping mall canal. There's an outside option, but it looked like you simply circle a pond. We had our photo taken at the 'Welcome to the Fabulous Las Vegas' sign (you'll find lots of friendly photographers here who will take your picture for a small tip – they are not official city staff though, so be careful who you give your camera to). We visited the white tigers and dolphins at the Mirage too (they are kept in such small enclosures I immediately wished we hadn't). You can also book helicopter tours of the Grand Canyon if you don't decide to drive there yourself, but again reserve in advance if you're not staying for long.

Despite Vegas being most famous for its casinos, we didn't spend long at all on the slot machines. Roulette and the other table games were expensive, so we didn't give them a go, although we did stay long enough to sample a few free drinks. Top tip, don't go to the bar; play a few slots and wait for the waitresses to bring you complimentary cocktails. Just remember they are only giving them to you in the hope that you'll get drunk and spend more money. You are also welcome to walk around any of the hotels and casinos if you just want to look.

The theatre was more up our street, and we can highly recommend *Las Vegas! The Show* (3663 S Las Vegas Blvd), which we booked upon arrival. A short bus ride will take you to the world's largest video screen, which showcases huge light displays each night at the Fremont Street Experience in downtown. Smoking isn't banned here, so it gets a little hazy at Fremont, which is under what is essentially a large tent across the street. There's also a giant zip wire, lots of casinos and places to drink, but Margaritaville inside the Flamingo Hotel and Casino (opposite Caesar's Palace) back on the strip was my favourite bar.

There are lots of restaurants in Vegas, but they are all pretty pricey, especially when they add an 18 per cent gratuity in some places. The restaurants inside Mandalay

Bay (a monorail ride away from the Luxor) are particularly steep, but the Rainforest Cafe in the MGM Grand was a lot of fun for breakfast. The gift shop is amazing – we bought a metre-long crocodile stuffed toy as our engagement present. We also celebrated in an adult-appropriate fashion by drinking an ice cold bottle of champagne in our room (thank you Karl and Gemma – Dave's brother and his wife).

Vegas was definitely an experience, but after a few days amongst replicas of world landmarks, we were keen to get back on the road. It was onto California, the final state of our trip.

9
CALIFORNIA'S MOST WANTED

On trips to the US, watching American TV is my guilty pleasure. I love the sensationalised news updates and the medication commercials that list an extraordinary collection of side effects. But as well as offering novelty in abundance, it also provides a vital source of information for road warriors traversing across state borders: the weather forecast.

From the moment we left Chicago, we'd been chasing torrential rain and flash floods. But bar the heavy downpours in Missouri and the crazy hail storm in Flagstaff (both of which made for some scary driving conditions), we'd pretty much managed to avoid the extreme weather wreaking havoc across America (cars had been swept away in Las Vegas floods days before we arrived at the strip). That was until we reached California.

Between Essex and Barstow, flooding had torn up the road surface and washed away bridges, leaving more than 100 miles of Route 66 completely impassable. Every time we tried to find a detour, we were met by 'road closed' signs and blockades across the tarmac. The interstate had got its revenge once again, and we were forced to surrender to the I-40.

The result was that we missed most of California's Mojave Desert stretch – one of the best drives on Historic Route 66 – instead picking up the road again after exit 179. But rather than lament on times that could have been in the final stage on our journey, I'll share with you the places we had planned to visit before we re-joined the highway just outside Victorville. You can fulfil our California dreams instead and make some memories of your own.

As much of the Mother Road travels through desert landscape here, make sure you stock up on water before you leave Arizona (or Nevada if you take the Las Vegas detour, where you'll pick up 66 again just before Goffs). Be careful of running out of gas too – much of this stretch is a string of forgotten ghost towns, so expect to look at more than you actually visit.

Even if you do have a full tank, you should still make time to stop at Roy's Cafe and Motel, a gas station and gift shop in Amboy. It's one of the most iconic buildings on all Route 66, famous for its gigantic neon sign and Googie architecture, a futurist style common between the 1940s and 1960s and inspired by the Space Age. The Googie movement was responsible for a whole collection of gas stations, motels and cafes that looked like they'd sprung from an episode of *The Jetsons*.

A former eatery and lodging, Roy's has appeared in countless films and American adverts (maybe even ones with a long list of medical side effects). In the 66 heyday, it employed 10 per cent of the town's residents, but business came to an abrupt halt the day I-40 opened, according to former proprietor Herman Burris.

Today Roy's, and the whole of Amboy, are owned by Albert Okura, who is working hard to restore it. Difficulty getting water in this part of California means the establishment no longer serves food or accepts overnight guests, but you should stop by for a photo and to purchase something from the store.

If it's food you're after, head to the Bagdad Cafe in Newbury Springs (60 miles from Amboy). The restaurant is famous for featuring in the 1987 German film of the same name, staring Marianne Sägebrecht, C. C. H. Pounder and Jack Palance. The place attracts movie fans by the coachload from across the world.

We were delighted to finally get back on Route 66 just before Lenwood, on a section of the road called the National Old Trails Highway. And this certainly went some way towards making up for our interstate ordeal; the road is full of rises and falls that make your stomach roll over as you bounce along. We finally stopped somewhere between Helendale and Victorville, ready to look at a field full of old glass.

The Bottle Tree Ranch is a spectacle that has to be seen to be believed. Housed behind a metal fence is a collection of rusting car parts, decaying road signs (including the rare 'turtle crossing' plaque), broken shotguns and even old toilet seats. The assortment of reclaimed junk sits on top of rows of trees constructed from brightly coloured glass bottles, which gleam in the sunshine to the sound of delicate wind chimes made of garbage.

At first, we were a little worried about just walking into this garden in the middle of nowhere, especially on account of the pack of dogs waiting for us at its gate. We soon realised the pooches were friendly and set about looking around the ranch. It wasn't long before we came across creator Elmer Long doing a spot of welding. He told us how he made the attraction unintentionally at first, using items he'd collected as a child when camping with his father.

But once he started, the forest kept growing. Now he

spends his days touring dumps and abandoned buildings looking for treasure to add to his collection. It's a sort of artistic recycling. The ranch attracts buses full of tourists – he'd already had 100 people visit him that day – and Elmer is busier than ever talking to them now the road is lively again, thanks to the resurgence of Route 66. As he spoke, a hummingbird hovered right next to his head – Elmer puts out sugar water for the birds every day, so they are as at home in his artificial forest as they would be in the real thing. The ranch is free to visit, although Elmer accepts donations, and is open from dawn until dusk every day. When we visited in the early evening, we were the only tourists around.

We left the attraction feeling positive about life. Despite the disappointing start to our day, we could feel good about humanity and the creative joy people bring each other. I think this might go some way to explain why we didn't drive off straight away when we arrived on the forecourt of our Victorville motel. Ready to unwind after a long day of driving, we didn't pay too much attention to its smashed windows, beat-up cars and the generally shady-looking characters walking around.

We thought nothing of it when our neighbour came to speak to Dave as I unpacked the Dodge – here was just another friendly Route 66 stranger, like the countless people we'd met at other motels on our journey. And, given that I desperately needed the loo and was busy trying to hide the fact I was a grown woman unpacking a three-foot stuffed crocodile out of the boot (so I could keep him safe in my motel room), I was happy to let them chat.

I couldn't make out the details of their conversation from where I was standing. However, the man seemed nice, asking Dave about why we were visiting the town. But then his questions became more focused on the Dodge. It was a lovely car. He'd sure love to go for a drive in it. He'd be happy to keep an eye on the vehicle if we wanted to go out for dinner, just to make sure it stayed safe, he said.

Did we want to know why he was staying here? He was on the run from the police. He used to be in a gang, he said. But then he won a million dollars. His wife had divorced him, taking most of the money, and now he was here with his new girlfriend, waiting for a pizza delivery, in the room next to us. A room he'd kitted out with cameras for his protection.

If Dave didn't believe him, the man said, he could look him up on the internet. Dave replied that he'd do so as soon as he got home – he hadn't brought his phone to the US (he lied). Don't worry, take this one, said the man as he reached into his car's glove box and took out one of a collection of broken phones from a ziplock bag. Dave thanked him and left for our room, leaving the cell on the truck's boot. Don't forget the phone, said the man, passing it to Dave.

We went swiftly to our room so I could finally use the loo, before walking straight back out (with the stuffed crocodile) and into reception to hand in a missing phone, along with our room keys. Thank you, but we wouldn't be staying.

We drove to a gas station, paranoid the man was following us in his truck, only to be accosted by some youths asking for gas money. We apologised and drove off. By this point it was dark and late. We were so freaked out that we decided the best thing to do would be to get out Victorville and forgo the last 97 miles of Route 66 to seek safety in LA. This meant we'd miss the original McDonald's in San Bernardino (now a museum run by the owner of Roy's, Amboy) and the second Wigwam Motel in Rialto (still taking bookings if you missed out on sleeping in a teepee in Holbrook). But that's the price we'd have to pay to feel safe. Luckily, the Ramada Plaza Hotel Suites West Hollywood on Santa Monica Boulevard (on Route 66 itself) could accommodate us. We checked in and headed straight to the 24-hour bar next door to calm our nerves.

When we were back in the UK, newspaper reports told us that Victorville ranked amongst California's top 10 most dangerous cities at the time, so we may have been justified in not sleeping the night. Do your research before you decide where to stay.

* * * *

If Los Angeles was a sandwich spread, it would be Marmite. You either love or hate the place. Despite friends warning us that we wouldn't like it, LA was actually one of our favourite cities on Route 66, and a fitting end to our journey.

However, you do need to prepare yourself. Los Angeles is like no other place you'll visit on your trip. There's little public transport, so you have to drive everywhere, and there is so much congestion; you'll spend a great deal of your time stuck in traffic. It's noisy and, although it doesn't look or feel dirty, your feet will be covered in soot by the end of the day if you venture out in sandals.

The drivers are crazy too. They will cut you up and pull out in front of you, and we saw a lot of vehicles with broken brake lights. It's the only time I've ever seen Dave truly stressed when driving (apart from when I didn't give him 'proper instructions' when navigating around Chelmsford back home). But they only drive erratically because everyone else does. It's the only way to actually get anywhere in such an overcrowded city.

When they're not driving, the people are lovely. The service is great and everyone seems to want to share their happiness with you. Maybe that's what happens when you live near so many beaches.

The actual end of Route 66 at Lincoln and Olympic Boulevard is disappointing. US law states that a highway can only end when another joins it, so it's a busy junction that would be unsafe to mark with a tourist attraction (although we drove to it anyway). But Santa Monica more than makes up for it with a choice of two different ways to celebrate reaching LA. The first, the Will Rodgers Highway Marker in Palisades Park, is simply a plaque on the ground. The second is the 'End of the Trail' sign on Santa Monica Pier and is far better if you only have time to visit one. It was placed there by Dan Rice, who owns the 66 to Cali gift stand next to it.

We'd first heard about Dan back in Missouri at the Gay Parita Service Station when Gary Turner made us promise that we visit him at the end of our trip. When we arrived at the stand near the end of the pier, Dan wasn't there. Instead we told his colleague all about our travels and the people that we'd met – Gary, Angel, Elmer, Melba the Mouth and so many more. In fact, we had so much to tell him that he didn't need to ask us the official quiz he usually puts to Route 66 roadies to prove they've really travelled its length. We'd done the Mother Road 'properly' and had earnt our certificates. You can get yours too, for a small fee of course. We celebrated with seafood and a game of whack-a-mole where I lost to a child. We then finished Route 66 as we'd started it in Chicago, with a Ferris wheel on the pier. But this time we were treated to a flock of pelicans flying by.

We packed a lot into our few days in LA. We took photos at the Beverly Hills sign (Beverly Gardens Park) and took a stroll down the famous Rodeo Drive shopping district. We spotted the names of our favourite celebs written in the stars on the Hollywood Walk of Fame and put our hand in the prints of the rich and famous outside Grauman's Chinese Theatre/TCL Chinese Theatre (both Hollywood Blvd). Written next to Robin Williams' hands is the inscription 'Carpe diem' – 'Seize the day'. He died the month before we left for America.

We saw the Hollywood Sign from the Griffith Observatory; it's no longer accessible by foot because of complaints from residents. We did have a good go at trying to reach it directly, but this only resulted in us getting a tad lost in the Hollywood Hills in a huge Dodge that was so long it only just survived the tight corners. We made it out in the end, but only because Dave noticed striking resemblances to the roads in *Grand Theft Auto* – he followed the routes he'd played in the game from memory. If it wasn't for being in a supercar, and thus at least looking a bit like we might have lived in the Hills, I don't think the residents would have been too happy with us invading their neighbourhood. So stick to the observatory – you can take in a show at the planetarium there too.

The Getty Center is also beautiful to see lit up at night and provides stunning views across the city, as well as some great works of art. We'd highly recommend booking onto the Warner Bros. Studio Tour before you travel (which we deemed the best of the available studios to visit), where you'll see sets from *Jurassic Park, True Blood* and the sound stage from *The Big Bang Theory*. If you do your research, they might even be filming when you go. Warner Bros. is also where *Friends* was filmed, so you'll have the chance to sit on the Central Perk sofa. Lunch or dinner at the SmokeHouse across from the lot (George Clooney's favourite restaurant apparently) is also well worth a visit.

When you leave for LAX (where we returned our car), make sure you leave plenty of time to negotiate the traffic. We didn't mind the queues in the end; when we got to the airport, our tickets were upgraded and we flew back business class. It was the perfect end to the holiday of a lifetime, even if I did get ill from too much free champagne…

* * * *

Life is a journey. Like Lillian Redman says, 'We are all travellers. From "birth till death," we travel between the eternities.' It's what you do with your time, and the people you do it with, that counts. And, to me, that's what driving the Mother Road is all about – adventure and experiences with those you love most.

So if you're looking for discovery, to learn something about history, culture and maybe even yourself, you best get booking those plane tickets. You owe it to yourself, and America's Main Street, to embark on the world's most famous road trip. Make Route 66 part of your own journey, meet its people and open your mind. May be you'll open theirs too.

Historic 66 is officially 2,448 miles long, but we travelled around 4,000 with our detours, and a few instances of getting lost. And I think about those miles nearly every day. That's why I wrote this book, and why Dave and I will be straight back there to do it all again as soon as we have the funds.

Your Route 66 adventure will never leave you, but it will give you memories to treasure forever.

ACKNOWLEDGEMENTS

I am forever grateful to the wonderful people who made this book, and my lifelong dream of publishing, a reality. No matter whether the parts they played in doing so were large or small, I have great pleasure in thanking them all.

Thank you to the talented and generous Christine Webster for her expertise. Thank you to Zoe Holmes of Fred Olsen Travel Agents for all her support when planning our trip, and to Carla Watkins and Darren David for giving me the confidence to see this book through. Not to forget Kylie Neuhaus from *Between England and Iowa* for her advice on self-publishing and one of my best friends, the gifted Dexter Harrison, for designing my logo.

Thank you to my amazing mum, Denise, for her continued encouragement and my fantastic dad, Andy, for helping to renovate our house so I had the time to write.

This guide would not have been possible without the vibrant attractions, motels and eateries of Route 66, and the dedicated people who run them each day. Thank you for your warmth, compassion and hospitality and for the work you do to ensure millions of travellers can enjoy the magic of the Mother Road. Melba, Elmer, Angel, Teresa, Nancy, Gary (RIP) and so many more to mention all by name – without you, there would be no *Brits on Route 66*, quite literally.

Jerry McClanahan's *EZ66 Guide for Travelers*, Michael Wallis's *Route 66 The Mother Road*, *Billy Connolly's Route 66* book and accompanying TV series, Tom Snyder's *Route 66 Traveler's Guide and Roadside Companion* and Henry Cole's *World's Greatest Motorcycle Rides* were all invaluable in researching our trip. Their books and documentaries are works of art – every Route 66 adventurer should own them. Thank you for igniting my passion for the Mother Road and the memories I'll treasure for a lifetime.

Thank you also to John Weiss for showing us around Adrian on that September day.

Most importantly, thank you to my travel buddy and loving husband, Dave, not just for driving me more than 2,500 miles across the States, but for supporting me to share our story. Thank you for 'giving' me the time to write this, for putting up with my wobbles, and for your advice and unconditional love. I love you millions – here's to many more adventures to come.

ABOUT THE AUTHOR

Vicki Graves is a British travel writer with an obsession for vintage Americana, mid-century design, Art Deco architecture and all things kitsch. So when she discovered that Route 66 is still alive and kicking, she found a kindred spirit - in the form of 2,448 miles of road between Chicago and LA. Vicki and her motor-mad husband got engaged on the highway and have been 66 super-fans ever since, passionate about helping people from across the world to drive the 'Main Street of America'.

Vicki also runs the *Brits on Route 66* blog (www.britsonroute66.co.uk), offering USA travel and lifestyle inspiration, recommendations for Americana events and attractions in the UK and plenty of ogle-worthy retro, kitsch and vintage.

WANT MORE BRITS ON ROUTE 66?

Follow my blog at www.britsonroute66.co.uk

There you'll find more Route 66 advice, USA travel and lifestyle inspiration, recommendations for Americana events and attractions in the UK and plenty of ogle-worthy retro, kitsch and vintage. And it's all written especially for those who live outside the USA – my Brits, Europeans and travellers across the globe who long to be on Route 66.

Printed in Great
Britain
by Amazon

32323013R00069